ARE YOU CONFU~~SED~~ ~~ABOUT~~ "HARDWARE," "SOFTWARE," "MODEM," "ROM," AND "RAM"?

ARE YOU WORRIED ABOUT HAVING TO LEARN COMPUTER LANGUAGES BEFORE YOU CAN EVEN MAKE YOUR COMPUTER WORK?

ARE YOU A COMPUTER GAME ADDICT LOOKING FOR THE ULTIMATE GAME SYSTEM?

ARE YOU WONDERING WHETHER A WORD PROCESSOR IS REALLY WORTH THE MONEY?

Whatever your needs and interests, whatever your questions about today's home computers, this guide will tell you all you want to know to make up your own mind and choose the computer that's right for you.

KEN USTON'S GUIDE TO HOME COMPUTERS

Technology Today and Tomorrow from MENTOR and SIGNET

(0451)

KEN USTON'S
GUIDE TO
HOME COMPUTERS

KEN USTON

A SIGNET BOOK

NEW AMERICAN LIBRARY

TIMES MIRROR

Copyright © 1983 by Ken Uston

All rights reserved

Many of the products listed herein are trademarks
of their respective manufacturers.

This book has been neither authorized nor endorsed by
any of the manufacturers whose names appear herein.

SIGNET, SIGNET CLASSIC, MENTOR, PLUME, MERIDIAN,
and NAL BOOKS are published by The New American Library, Inc.,
1633 Broadway, New York, New York 10019

First Printing, August, 1983

1   2   3   4   5   6   7   8   9

PRINTED IN THE UNITED STATES OF AMERICA

*To the three people
who made this book possible:*

Inga · Love
David Ahl · Knowledge and friendship
Erroll Garner · Soul

Acknowledgments

It would have been tough, if not impossible, to complete this book without the cooperation of David Ahl, founder and editor-in-chief of *Creative Computing* magazine. David generously allowed me to roam freely around his magazine offices, working with his many computers and hundreds of software packages. I'm also grateful to David for helping fill what few leisure hours we had, playing countless computer games at his house.

My thanks to Betsy Staples, the tireless editor of *Creative Computing*, and to the other "Creative" people, including Owen Linzmayer, John Anderson, Bill Bauman, and Ron Antonaccio.

Thanks to Katie Uston for helping to revise the manuscript and assisting in some of the research. My gratitude and love to Inga for putting up with months of research and writing at hotels all over the country, much of which took place at very weird times of the day (and night).

And, as always, thanks to Erroll Garner for providing me daily pleasure...through his music and mine.

Contents

SECTION I
WHAT CAN HOME COMPUTERS DO—
SPECIFICALLY?

SECTION II
WHICH COMPUTER IS FOR YOU?

A Note to the Reader

The first question I asked myself before deciding whether to write this book was: "Is it needed?"

I was on a tour while the idea for a book on home computers was germinating. I visited bookstores from coast to coast and saw a few "introductory" books interspersed among enormous numbers of technical texts.

I bought (and tried to read) every one I could find. Naturally when you're thinking about writing a book, you want to see what's out there.

The books had titles that implied that they were simple—you know, computers for the layman, computers in everyday language, computers made simple, that kind of stuff. And just about every one I read wasn't for the layman, wasn't in everyday language, and wasn't simple. So I decided to write this book.

This book is for those who want to buy a computer and use it as they would, say, a microwave oven. When most of us buy an appliance, we want to plug it in, use it with a minimum of fuss and bother, and enjoy the results. We couldn't care less how a microwave oven works—as long as it does the job.

It *is* possible to use a computer this way. But most people don't know that yet.

More mystery surrounds home computers than just about any other appliance, understandably so.

—We've heard about "programming" and assume we have to know how to do that to use a computer. No way!

—We've overheard people talking about some weird new "language" called BASIC that sounds far from

1

basic. Or maybe we've run into terms like "eproms," "loops," and "prompts," which were intimidating because we knew they didn't refer to dances, knots, and early birds.

Forget it! You don't need to know any of that stuff. Not even close! You can use a computer just as you use a vacuum cleaner, a television set, or a car.

Here's another example: Last year, I must have rented forty cars from Hertz. There were many different models (just like computers). I don't know (or want to know) the difference between a thermostat and a distributor—to say nothing of trying to find them under the hood (are distributors under the hood?). Computers can be used in the same way.

The home computer *does* have a place in the lives of some—not all—of us. But there are few objective sources to tell you why and how—for several reasons:

1. The computer ads we see every day obviously have an ax to grind. Their message: "Buy a computer from us."

2. The salesmen in Sears, K-Mart, Radio Shack®, and computer stores have an ax to grind. Their message: "Buy a computer from us."

3. The industry is complicated; the choices are many. Most computer salesmen don't know the answers. Worse yet, sometimes they guess (who wants to admit that he doesn't know enough about his job?).

4. Most people who know about computers talk a very odd language—a computerese which prevents them from communicating with the rest of us. Some live, eat, and breathe computers. Terms like "conducer," "microprocessor," and "I/O bus" have become commonplace to them. They come to think that everyone understands them. Others talk this way because it shows how much they know.

It's strange. Here we have probably the fastest-growing home appliance. It was even named *Time* magazine's 1982 Machine of the Year. Yet a question we hear again and again, even in some of the computer magazines, is: "What can home computers *really* do—other than allow us to play video games?"

Why is this? One reason is that the word isn't getting out clearly.

What This Book Will Not Do

1. Try to convince you that you need a home computer. Most books written about computers are by people who are really sold on them. They come out with what are called "gee whiz" books. They go on and on about the miraculous things home computers can do. If home computers are so wonderful, why are so many of them gathering dust in closets, basements, and garages?

2. Tell you how a computer (or a television, or a tape recorder, or a microwave oven) works. I'll leave terms like "binary," "memory cycles," and "hexadecimal" to the technicians.

3. Relate the history of computers. Again, I'll tell you how to use a computer without knowing anything (or as little as possible). The history of computers (or television, tape recorders, or microwave ovens) can be found elsewhere.

Who This Book Is For

1. You've been hearing a lot about home computers lately. You've read about how they can just about make

your bed, tie your shoes, mow the lawn, and tuck you in at night. You're skeptical (rightly so), but wonder, "Is it conceivable that I might ever benefit from one?" You'd like to know what they *really* can and cannot do.

2. You're fairly well convinced that a computer can help you at home—or you just want to get one, for whatever reason. You've read all the standard advice (first determine your needs, don't buy solely on price, talk to friends who know about computers, visit the computer stores, etc.) But you'd like someone to do the research for you—someone who will tell you, in plain English, what the various brands can and cannot do and which one most likely is for you.

3. You're into video games and know about the Atari® VCS™ and Intellivision™. You know that home computers play games, too. You'd like a comparison between all the video systems and the game-playing home computers. You also wonder which provides the ultimate game system.

4. You own a home computer. You feel guilty because it's gathering dust. You'd like to learn how to use it without reading some manual you have to translate into English.

When you finish this book:

1. You'll know whether a home computer is for you. If it is, you'll know which one(s) you should look at first. If it's not, you'll know why not.

2. You'll know what to look for in buying computers and programs, whether you're shopping now or in the future—i.e., you'll be a "smart consumer."

3. You'll know how to use a home computer and get the most out of it.

4. You'll be able to say, "Finally, I understand!"

Introduction

When television entered our lives, some new terms came with it—like "channel," "horizontal hold," and "fine tuning." We needed to know these terms so we could use the TV.

Other terms also came with it—like "transducer" and "transformer." These are terms we didn't need to know to use the TV.

It's the same with computers. There are a few words you should know, words that will be commonplace in a few years. I'll introduce most of them in this chapter. And don't worry: There are only a few in this entire book.

The words will be "defined" with you in mind. They're explained in plain English, not complicated computer terminology.

Three words that you should know (they are rapidly becoming household words) are "hardware," "program," and "software."

Hardware refers to the actual computer equipment, the "hard" stuff that you can rap your knuckles on.

Programs are sets of instructions that tell the computer what to do.

Software refers to the programs that are "run" on the computer.

An often-used, and good, analogy compares computers to stereo sets. The hardware comprises the amplifier, the turntable, and the speakers. The software consists of the records and cassettes. You "play" records; you "run" programs.

Let's take this analogy between stereos and computers one step further. In a stereo system, the guts of the system, the amplifier, could be considered the "brains." It miraculously translates your record or cassette tape into sound.

Input is what is put in. To put music into the stereo, we use "input" devices, such as turntables, cassette tape players, or eight-track decks.

Output is what comes out. In a stereo system, the output—music—is put out on the speakers, the "output" devices.

With a computer, the computer itself is the brains. The input can come from several sources, and the output can take several forms:

Cassette tape recorders. These are just like the

ones used in stereo systems. The difference is that information (mostly letters and numbers), rather than prerecorded music, is being "read" into the computer.

Disk drives. These read information from disks, just as turntables "read" music from records.

There are two basic types of disks:

Floppy disks. Information can be held on little bend-able pieces of plastic that look a lot like 45-rpm records. They're called "floppy disks," floppy because they bend, disks because they're round (although they look square in their little envelopes). They're also called "diskettes" because they're small, about 5 inches in diameter.

Hard disks. Information can also be stored on much larger disks, made from metal. They require their own disk drives. But forget about these hard disks;

they are for heavy users, mostly in business. They're not for us.

Keyboards. Most keyboards look just like a typewriter. We use keyboards to enter data into the computer. If we're writing, we type our text in; if we're doing calculations, we enter numerical data.

Monitors. The output from a computer is shown on a screen—usually our TV screen, just as with the video game systems. Screens are also made specifically for computer use. These are called "monitors" (don't ask me why; I would think "display" or "screen" might be more apt, but that would probably be too simple).

Monitors are like TVs. They can either be in color (a "color monitor") or in black and white (computer people call these "monochrome monitors," because the information is shown in one color; the color actually can be black, white, green, or something else).

Printer. If we want to get information on a piece of paper (computerists call this "hard copy"—we can forget that term), we need to have the information printed. What do we use? You guessed it—a printer. There are two types of printers:

Dot-matrix printer (less expensive). The characters are made up of little dots. The characters are usually totally readable, but they're not as sharp and crisp as those of a good typewriter; you usually see the little dots. It's great for term papers, personal letters, and informal writing.

Letter-quality printer (more expensive). The print looks just like that produced by a good typewriter— solid characters, instead of dots. This is what you'd

probably want for résumés, business letters, and book manuscripts.

Daisy-wheel printer. This is a type of letter-quality printer. It's given this strange name because it has daisy-shaped objects (with petals) which form the characters.

Modem. As you'll soon find out, you can get information from huge storehouses of data over the telephone (for a fee, of course). But to hook up your computer to such sources, you attach to the computer a device that is also tied to your phone. This is called a "modem." I won't bore you with why it's called that—it's technical.

There are only three more terms to learn: "ROM," "RAM," and "K." You'll encounter these terms almost immediately when shopping for a computer.

ROM refers to the permanent instructions inside the computer that tell it to get going (somewhat like whatever it is in a stereo that tells the arm where to place the stylus when playing 45-rpm records as opposed to 33-rpm records). There are different sizes of ROM, but the size of (and actually even the definition of) ROM is not of great concern to the average person shopping for a home computer.

RAM—that is, "usable" RAM—refers to the portion of computer memory that can be used to run your programs. You *are* concerned with the size of usable RAM. RAM is measured in something called "K."

K is a measure of capacity—like horsepower in a car or cubic feet in a refrigerator. A computer with 2K RAM is severely limited; one with 64K is more than adequate for most home uses. We'll be far more specific about K in Section II.

Would you believe, that's it! You need know no more fancy words to learn to use computers. I told you it would be easy!

Now let's discuss how we're going to accomplish what was promised in "A Note to the Reader." We're going to do it in two steps:

Section I: What Can Home Computers Do—Specifically?

We describe in detail what programs can do for you in the categories you're most likely to be interested in. We discuss specific programs, how you use them, and what benefits they provide. The categories are:

1. Home finance—like balancing your checkbook, keeping a budget, and figuring your taxes (a few of us do the first two; most of us do the third).

2. What computers can do to help us write (the computer people call it "word processing").

3. Education—how computers help us learn things, and what things. And I'm not just talking about kids.

4. Financial spreadsheets. There are programs called "calcs" that some of us may find useful for "crunching" numbers; others will find them a crashing bore.

5. Information. There's a lot of data we can get into our home by tying our computer to what they call "data bases." This varies from the contents of an up-to-date encyclopedia and stock-market quotations to reviews of movies, books, and restaurants.

6. Games. There are hundreds of home computer games, some quite boring, others totally addictive. We'll discuss the types of games you can play on computers and which computers do the best job of satisfying your video-game needs.

7. Other entertainment—how computers can be a fourth (and second and third) for bridge or a worthy opponent (and instructor) in chess, checkers, blackjack, backgammon, and other games.

8. How computers can help us write and arrange music, create art, and file and retrieve all kinds of information like Christmas lists and recipes, and help us diet or exercise.

9. How to find the programs you need to make your computer do what you want.

When you're through with this, you'll know what you can do with a home computer whether you spend just a few hundred dollars on one (they're getting cheaper all the time) or several thousand.

It's up to you to determine if these uses are for you. Some of them may seem trivial or pointless—what good is it to balance your checkbook on a computer if you never balance your checkbook anyway? Others may be things you wish you could do now, and you'll want to run out and buy a computer tomorrow.

Section II: Which Computer Is for You?

In this section, we look at each of the home computers you're likely to consider. You'll learn the good and bad points of each, and other features that may turn you on or turn you off.

At the end, we talk about which computers do which things best—by brand name. So if you read Section I first and found a few things you like, Section II will tell you which computers can do these things best. And we get *very* specific.

How Can You Keep Up-to-Date? What Does the Future Hold?

The home computer field is so dynamic that developments occur literally on a day-by-day basis. The appendix to this book, "Periodicals That Can Keep You Up-to-Date," explains how to keep track of what's going on and gives a brief clue as to what is likely to happen.

That's it. As I said, when you finish this book, you should know:

—what a computer can do,
—what a computer cannot do,
—whether you want a computer to work for you,
—if so, which one you probably should choose, and
—which computers (or video systems) you'll most enjoy playing games on.

SECTION I

WHAT CAN HOME COMPUTERS DO— SPECIFICALLY?

As I said, "software" refers to the many programs that make your computer run. There was no generally available software for home computers just a few years ago (there wasn't even a home computer until 1975). But that's no longer true. Two million home computers were shipped by manufacturers in 1982. Industry analysts estimate six million will be shipped in 1983. Companies realize that there's a lot of money in supplying us with programs to run on these computers.

The software market is exploding. Even the biggest computer cynic would have been convinced of this after a quick stroll through the January 1983 Consumer Electronics Show.

Companies are stumbling over themselves to come up with new game ideas, to make education fun, to make it easy for us to keep our personal finances on a computer, to allow us to write on a computer, and to link our computer with major information sources around the country. In some cases, they've succeeded; in others, they've failed dismally.

This section tells you what's out there. Most books that cover this subject are general. They tell you that you can keep a budget on a computer—period. They provide nothing on how the program works or what is required of you. They tell you that Johnny can learn English, but don't explain how.

I've gotten specific in this section, explaining the programs in some detail. I've done this so you'll know precisely *how* the programs work, and what you have to do to use them. Remember, you don't have to know how to program the computer. All you usually have to do is type in some basic information—or operate a game controller.

This section has eight chapters that explain how software can help you in various home functions. At the end of the section, a final chapter discusses how to buy software. This subject is quite important, because many of the thousands of software packages available are far from cheap, and their quality ranges from terrible to impressive.

Chapter 1

Home Finance: Checkbooks, Budgets, Taxes and Personal Finance

Checkbooks and Budgets

Software companies are trying to convince us that we need their products to balance our checkbooks and keep personal budgets. I believe the value of many of these kinds of programs is questionable.

Many of us just don't balance our checkbook. We rely, right or wrong, on the accuracy of the bank computers. Even if we do balance our checkbook, it's such a trivial task that it's silly to do it on a computer. Similarly, we may not want to keep a budget. Either we choose not to regulate our lives to that extent or we find budgeting impractical or unnecessary.

Some new computer owners will get all excited about their computer budget and faithfully record the data for a month or two, then grow weary of the process. The result: The good intentions have resulted in an unused $40 program, and the computer is used once again only to play *Donkey Kong*™ or *Asteroids*™.

Budget programs can run on the smaller computers. Some form of data storage device is required, the cheapest being a cassette recorder. Some programs do both checkbook balancing and budgeting at the same time. Budget programs may be of value to you if:

—You really do want to keep a budget, but wouldn't know how to set one up if your life depended on it.

—You need a shot of self-discipline to get started in setting up a budget.

—You spend hours, at the end of the year, sorting checks and cross-totaling them for income tax or other purposes.

There are a number of checkbook/budget packages available for each of the more popular home computers. In many cases, these two functions are combined into one program. Some are inadequate; some, average; and a few, excellent.

You've probably read a dozen times that computers can keep a budget and wondered, "Yeah, but how?" To show you how, I'll use, as an illustration, a fairly good package put out by Radio Shack® for its TRS-80® Color Computer. It costs $40, and a cassette recorder is required. The program is called *Personal Finance*.

1. First you set up a budget, by categories. The program has common preselected expense categories, such as auto, clothing, rent, food, and gas. You may select them merely by hitting a key on the keyboard. If your spending habits are not in tune with what the Radio Shack people assume to be the typical American household, you may change these categories by typing in anything you choose (such as pet snakes, Cutty Sark, Picasso paintings, or computer software).

2. You type in the amount you plan (or hope) to spend on each budget category each month. If you know the rent is going to be $400 a month, every month, you can tell the computer that, without having to enter it twelve times.

3. You type in information about your bank account(s), including name of bank and beginning balance. You may enter data for up to nine accounts.

4. Every month, when you get your canceled checks, you enter the budget category and the amount into

the computer. For credit-card payments, you can make several entries, if more than one expense category is involved.

5. The computer tells you what your bank balances are (it shades the figure on the screen, if you're over-drawn).

At the end of every month, you have a review of your financial picture for the month that looks something like this:

BUDGET CATEGORY	BUDGETED $	$ SPENT	DIFFERENCE
Rent	$450	$450	$ 0
Automobile	130	180	+50
Clothing	150	80	-70
etc.			

This may be helpful in detecting where you've spent too much (or budgeted too little). You can then make adjustments in your spending habits, your budget, or both.

At the end of the year (or whenever you want), you can get a summary of your expenses in each category, that looks something like this:

Category Entertainment			
MONTH	BUDGETED $	ACTUALLY SPENT	DIFFERENCE
Jan.	$ 165	$ 142	$ -23
Feb.	165	180	+15
March	165	265	+100
....			
Dec.	165	365	+200
Year 1983	$1,980	$2,100	$+120
Year average	165	175	+10

For each category the computer adds the total spent for the year and gives you the monthly average. This could be of value in preparing tax data and in setting up a budget for the following year.

Timex® 1000™ Checkbook Programs

A listing of programming instructions for a checkbook program for the Timex 1000 is contained in *The Timex Personal Computer Made Simple* (Signet Books, 1982, page 94). The program balances your checkbook, but for the life of me I fail to see why anyone would want to do it this way. It's far easier to calculate the balance in your checkbook either manually or with a $10 calculator.

Timex itself sells checkbook and home finance cassettes, but these programs (*The Checkbook Manager* and *The Budgeter*) are too simple to be of any practical value in budgeting.

Household Budget Management™— Texas Instruments

Texas Instruments sells a program for its TI-99/4A™ computer called *Household Budget Management*™, which is used with a cassette tape or other storage device. When the program is loaded, four options appear on the screen:

1. See Demo Data (demonstrates the program)
2. Set Up Budget for 1st Time
3. Load Your Data
4. Start a New Budget Year

As in the budget program for the TRS-80 Color Computer (Coco), you may either use preset expense categories or enter your own. You type in your budget (by month) and actual expenses as they're incurred or at the end of the month. You have your choice of several financial analyses:

1. Budget and actual expenses in all categories, for a single month or year-to-date

2. Budget and actual expenses for each category, by month

3. A comparison of total income and expenses (budget versus actual)

The program automatically calculates the percentage difference between actual and budgeted amounts and draws colored bar charts on the screen.

Household Budget Management does not include checkbook balancing. Further, it is set up so that only a few expense categories can be seen on the screen at one time.

Commodore VIC 20™ Programs

A program called *Checkbook*™ (MIS, Boulder Creek, CA) allows the VIC 20 computer to record check transactions and balances your checking account. It also searches and totals all checks written to a given payee (including "cash"). I doubt if *Checkbook* will prove of value to the average family. It might be useful to those who write hundreds of checks each year and must summarize them by payee.

Commodore produces personal finance cartridges for the VIC 20 which organize and analyze personal expenses. I don't recommend them because they're not comprehensive enough to be of use to the average household.

An Atari® Budget Program
That Doesn't Balance Checkbooks

Atari has an average program, called *Home Financial Management*™, that is contained on a cassette and is entered into the computer using a cassette recorder. You select budget categories from a list of 50 provided by the program, or you may type in your own. The program can handle up to 30 expenses categories with a 16K computer (125 categories with 24K, and 200 categories with 32K or more). Data analysis includes income and expenses by category, by month, or year-to-date. It also shows you "cash flow" (income less expenses) by month. The program shows beginning and ending cash flow balances. Bar charts, comparing budget and actual amounts, are displayed on the screen. If you have a printer, you can get copies of the data.

The Best Budget Program I've Seen

The best home finance package I've encountered is *The Home Accountant*™ (Continental Software, Los Angeles, CA). The program costs $75 and runs on Atari, Apple®, IBM® PC™, and Commodore 64™ computers. 48K and a disk drive are required. The program balances up to five checking accounts and handles dozens of budget categories. You may also label each transaction separately to get helpful summaries at the end of the period. *The Home Accountant* has several other helpful features:

1. If you have a printer, it can print checks.
2. It prepares a net worth statement and an income and expense statement.

3. It can help in keeping track of amounts outstanding. For example, if you write a check to your VISA account, the program debits your checking account and credits your VISA account.

4. It creates bar charts of income and expense. It also plots, on a graph, up to three budget categories at a time, with trend lines.

Income Tax Preparation

There are several programs that prepare federal income taxes. They are fairly complex and require large amounts of computer memory, usually 48K or more.

People with simple tax situations won't find these programs practical. They're not for those who take the standard deduction. They're probably not of value to those who itemize but have relatively simple returns. Many of those with complicated returns will probably prefer to continue using a tax accountant, for peace of mind and to avoid getting directly involved in the details of tax preparation.

One income tax preparation program is *E-Z Tax*™ (E-ZTAX, San Jose, CA), which sells for $70. You type in answers to questions that the program asks, and it computes your tax and prints the tax forms. *E-Z Tax* can accommodate the needs of most taxpayers. It prepares Form 1040 and Schedules A, B, C, D, E, F and G, to name just a few.

The program runs on Apple II™ (48K), IBM PC (64K), and Atari computers, and requires a disk drive and printer. Users are provided a 24-hour toll-free number to call with questions.

Home Tax™ (Learning Shack, Irvine, CA) also prepares income tax returns (cost: $97). It asks you pertinent questions, and you type in the answers. When it knows all it needs to know, it calculates your taxes and prints the tax forms. To reflect changes in tax laws, users are promised updated annual diskettes at "a nominal charge." *Home Tax* runs on the Apple II (48K required).

Most of us will probably not benefit from home computer tax preparation. If you do decide to go that route, however, the cost of the software is totally deductible, and a portion of the cost of your computer system may also be deductible. There's even a free program which will have your computer calculate your deduction for buying the computer (program listing in *Popular Computing* magazine, December 1982, page 59).

Investments

Computers can help investors in the stock market in basically three ways:

1. Record-keeping. The user may enter in the stocks he owns, with current prices and other data relating to purchases, sales, commissions, and dividends. He is provided with the value of his holdings, profit or loss, and comparison of how well he did compared to such barometers as the Dow Jones Index.

2. Analysis. Computer programs make it possible to analyze common stocks, options, commodities, or other investments in ways that would be impossible to do manually.

3. Financial information. The Dow Jones News/Re-

trieval Service, probably the best-known service (see Chapter 5), provides exhaustive information on thousands of securities. There are programs that provide access to this service, retrieve information, and automatically compute values of portfolios. It is possible to establish earnings or performance criteria and search through the entire Dow Jones data base to get listings of those that meet the criteria. This list can then be further analyzed, using more detailed computer programs, to help in making buying decisions.

Some of the better investment programs:

Dow Jones Market Analyzer™ (Dow Jones Co., Princeton, NJ) is not cheap ($250), but it provides exhaustive analyses of common stocks for the Apple II. It can prepare over a dozen different kinds of charts for each stock, preparing trend lines, moving averages, and semi-logarithmic plotting.

The Personal Investor™ (PBL Corporation, Wayzata, NM), also for the Apple II (48K, disk driver, and modem), ties in with the Dow Jones Service as well. It retrieves information on the user's portfolio (or other stocks) and prepares summaries of portfolios, profit and loss information, and dividend data.

Stock Option Analysis Program™ (H&H Scientific, Fort Washington, MD) retrieves information from the Dow Jones Service (Apple II). It analyzes and predicts prices of stock options, considering the price of the common stock and the period of time remaining before the option expires.

Stock Charting™ is a program for the Atari 800™ (24K). You type in information on common stocks, and the program prepares a 120-day graph of the stock price. Other information is also shown, including price-earnings ratios, yields, dividends, and moving averages.

Other Home Finance Programs

There are numerous other home finance programs that do everything from keeping track of your auto expenses to helping you with your newspaper route. While much of this software is oversimplified or of limited practical use, some programs might prove helpful, depending upon your interests.

Here's a brief sampling:

Programs that help in buying a house, a car, or other major items are available for all the home computers. Some perform computations that could be done just as easily with a calculator; others are more refined.

A "free" program available for the Timex 1000 computes monthly payments on a car or house, given the total sales price, down payment, and interest rate (listed in *The Timex Personal Computer Made Simple*, Signet, December 1982). This program uses the computer as a hand-held calculator. A somewhat more complex program for the VIC 20 is called *Loan & Mortgage Calculator*™.

ViCalc™ (for the VIC 20—UMI Software) allows you to make calculations rapidly. You may use any of 14 registers displayed on the screen and tie them together mathematically. The program allows you to use the standard arithmetic functions, exponents, and trigonometric operations (such as sine or cosine). If you enter the amount of a loan, the interest rate, and the monthly payments, *ViCalc* computes the amount of interest you pay each month.

A number of programs may be useful to treasurers of clubs or those in charge of preparing income and expense statements for organizations such as churches or PTΛs. One, written for the Coco, calculates and prints financial summaries, listings of income and expense, and a summary of checks written. This program is free (listed in *80 Micro*, January 1983, page 227). The typing of the program instructions will be a laborious task, however. Club treasurers might also find some of the better budget programs mentioned earlier useful.

Texas Instruments has a potentially helpful program for the TI-99/4A called *Home Financial Decisions*™. It goes a step or two beyond the hand calculator and analyzes financial data in four areas: loans, residence, car, and savings. Here's a listing of the alternatives that appear on the screen, to give you an idea of the scope of this package:

Loans:
—size of payments
—size of the down payment
—number of payments
—amount you can borrow
—cost of early payoff
Residence:
—cost of buying a house
—buying house A or B
—remain in present house or buy new one
—remain in house or rent
—cost of refinancing a mortgage
Car:
—buy a car
—buy car A or B
—lease or buy car
—keep car or buy new one
—keep or lease car
Savings:
—future amount in account

—size of deposits to reach goal
—amount of time to reach goal
—amount needed for regular withdrawal (i.e., how much is needed in your savings account to draw out $X for Y months).

There's a program (Atari Program Exchange [APX], Sunnyvale, CA) that keeps track of gasoline and other expenses for up to six cars. Personally I think this program is a solution in search of a problem.

APX also offers *Newspaper Route Management*, which keeps track of up to a hundred newspaper customers. It records customer name, address, and whether he is a weekday, Sunday, or seven-day customer. I think I'd still prefer to use the good old payment book that I had when doing my paper route.

Several loan mortgage analysis programs are available for the Atari, including *Loan Analyser*™ (Creative Software) and *Decision Maker* (APX).

For real estate investors (or speculators), there are programs to keep track of your investments. One excellent program, for the Apple IIe™ and IBM PC, is *Real Estate Analyzer*™ (Howard Software Services, La Jolla, CA). You supply the computer with all kinds of details (loan information, depreciation data, market values, lease income, and expenses). You may even input separate inflation rates for your properties, your expenses, and rental income. *Real Estate Analyzer* gives you cash flow reports, return on investment, and various rates of return.

Chapter 2

Word Processing:
Using a Computer to Write

Video games are addictive. So is word processing. Once you write for a while on a word processor (to save space, I'll refer to word processing occasionally as WP), you're spoiled; it's tough to go back to a typewriter.

Don't get me wrong. I'm not trying to sell you on word processing. But I do want you to get a feel for what it's really like.

The very first time I sat down and wrote on a computer using a word processing program, a friend helped me get through the basic steps to be able to use it. Personal instruction is the way to go. You'll learn in minutes what might take hours searching through an instruction manual.

The first thing you learn to do is move a "cursor" (a little character that tells you where you are in the text) left, right, up, and down.

You'll soon discover the "delete" key, which, I believe, is phenomenal. When it's struck, a character (usually the one over the cursor or to the immediate left of the cursor) disappears. If the key is held down, a series of characters (in most WP programs) is deleted, so that several letters or words are automatically "erased." There are even easier ways to delete longer portions of text, which we'll discuss later.

WP eliminates the need to hit the return key. Using a computer, the writer just keeps typing; the computer takes care of going to the next line automatically. This eliminates a typestroke every sixty strokes or so, to say nothing of the wait while the carriage or type ball returns to the left-hand position.

The writer need not worry about reaching the end of a page. When typing I often get preoccupied with writing and type several lines after the page has ended, lines which then have to be retyped. WP removes this problem. And, of course, the time-consuming process of changing the paper is eliminated.

Some WP programs have a centering option, which saves time. You can type a heading, hit a key or two, and *voilà*, the heading is centered with computer accuracy.

Word processing offers other advantages:

1. Editing and reediting become easy. No longer do you ask yourself, "Is making that change worth retyping the whole page?" You become much more willing to improve a piece of writing using word processing. Once the changes are made, you can sit back and let the printer do the work.

2. Most word processing programs permit "block moves," which, as you might have guessed, move blocks of text from place to place. This does away with the old cut-and-paste bit. Block moves can save typing in another way. For example, in Chapter 20, I list 11 computers several times. I typed the list only once, and block-moved the original whenever the list was needed.

3. Search-and-replace is a feature included in most word processing programs. The computer is told to look for a word throughout the text and replace it with another one. Say you wrote a novel that took place in Hoboken, and you want to change the location to Montgomery. Search-and-replace will find

every "Hoboken" and replace it with "Montgomery."
Another example: Say you're writing a book about
gas chromatographs. To save time, you can type "G"
whenever you mean "gas chromatograph," and automatically make the substitutions later.

4. Silence, darkness, and comfort. Two years ago,
I lived at a hotel in New York City for two months,
writing a book on a typewriter. I tried to work during
"normal" hours to avoid bothering other guests with
my clacking. Computer writing is so quiet that I can
work any time of day or night and disturb no one.
Even when someone else is sleeping in the same room,
I can keep working, because I can write with the lights
dim (the computer screen is self-lit).

With WP, you can work sitting in an armchair or
sitting on a couch, if the keyboard is of the detachable
type. In doing research, you can lie in bed, read periodicals or books, or just think and type ideas into
the computer, without even looking at the screen.

5. Much work can be avoided by saving key letters,
names and addresses, table formats, or lists of things
on disks. The information can be called up whenever
it's needed. For example, in doing this book, I wrote
to numerous manufacturers for information, copies
of software, and so on. I wrote basically one standard
letter and made minor changes as appropriate; the
WP took the drudgery out of the task of sending out
so many nearly identical letters.

6. Many word processors number pages automatically; some repeat a heading on the top of each page
(the way many legal documents do). Most allow you
to underline and to use boldface; the latter is not
possible on most typewriters.

7. Have you ever had to count the words in something you wrote, for example when the teacher said

an essay had to be 1,000 words or the publisher wanted a 4,000-word article? Many programs count the words for you automatically.

What I Don't Like About Word Processing

The biggest problem with word processing is that if something goes wrong, it *really* goes wrong. It can make a grown man cry, or at least swear a lot.

Picture toiling over a couple thousand words of prose. You're caught up in the creative process. You keep working, not wanting to interrupt your flow of literature to do something as mundane as transfer data to a disk for safekeeping.

Suddenly, Fido runs by and somehow manages to pull out the computer plug. Your work has vanished into thin air. It's as if you'd never done it. After you've strangled the dog, you've got to sit down and do it all over again.

Or imagine having written even more—35 pages or so. But you're no dummy. Every five pages, you carefully saved your work onto a disk. When you're finally finished, boy, do you feel good. You happily take the disk out of the disk drive.

In your exuberance, you drop the disk on the floor. It lands in a little pool of catsup that dripped down from the hamburger you ate on a break, three hours and 14 pages ago. I won't even finish the story—it's too sad.

Or you just composed a little gem and decide to print it immediately. But you want to put something from another disk in front of it. You open the disk drive. The phone rings. You make a date Saturday night with someone you've been wanting to go out with for a month. Wow!

You hang up. OK. Where were we? Oh, yes—printing. You push the keys to print what's in the computer. You hear strange noises. What happened? My God! The door to the disk drive is open! You forgot to take out the original disk and put in the second disk. It's rewrite time.

I'm chicken. I hate the thought of redoing something I've already sweated over. I copy and recopy disks. I save and resave text. I print and reprint documents.

As a result, I often have so many disks and piles of paper that I forget where the most recent material is. I forget what text is on which disk, and so on. Obviously, it takes careful organization, labeling, filing, and so on, to be totally safe. But aren't those the very chores that computers are supposed to help us avoid?

There are minor irritations, too. When you're zapping along at a good clip and reach the end of a line, it often happens in several popular WP programs that letters are dropped. The computer apparently gets preoccupied; it's thinking about changing lines. I'm now becoming reconciled to the extra editing needed to correct these omissions. But that doesn't mean I like it.

There are other pitfalls. The special keys to be hit on one word processing program I used were quite similar for two different functions—one was inserting a character, the second was deleting a line. When you inadvertently delete a line you actually wanted, you get mad. When you do it 30 times, you get very mad.

But don't get me wrong. I think word processing is a big improvement over the typewriter. (I must admit, though, that even today I do quite a bit of writing on a typewriter. There *is* something to be said for creating letters on a piece of paper before your very eyes, rather than having to wait for the disk to be processed by a printer.)

Some Word Processing Programs

Unusual care is required in selecting a word processing program:

1. Price variations are extreme (some sell for $14.95; others cost $500).

2. The effectiveness of WP programs varies widely, sometimes in inverse proportion to price.

3. There is no program that can run on all computers.

Once again, we get what we pay for. It's difficult to get good word processing on low-priced computers (e.g., the VIC 20™, Coco, TI-99/4A™, or Atari® 400™). Word processing on these systems is recommended only for the infrequent writer. Here are several that are available:

Timex Sinclair 1000™: Yes, there are word processing programs for this tiny computer with the membrane keyboard. Two are called *ZTEXT* and *LTEXT* ; they sell for $14.95 (Oasis Software, Weston Super Mare, England). Because of the limitations of the Timex 1000 (see Chapter 10), these programs are not recommended, to say the least.

VIC 20: *Wordcraft* (United Microwave Industries, Pomona, CA) and *Quick Brown Fox*™ (Quick Brown Fox, New York, NY).

TRS-80® Color Computer: *Telewriter*™ (Cognitec, Del Mar, CA), *Super Color Writer II* (Nelson Software, Minneapolis, MN), and *Color Scripsit*™ (Radio Shack).

Atari: *Letter Writer*™ ($19 from CE Software, Chicopee, MA) and *Mini-Processor* ($15 from Santa Cruz Educational Software, Soquel, CA) are at the low end. *The Atari Word Processor*™ ($150 from Atari) and *Letter Perfect*™ ($140 from LJK Enterprises, St. Louis, MO) are more acceptable.

Apple II™: *The Executive Secretary*™ (Personal Business Systems, Minneapolis, MN) and *Apple Writer*™ (Apple Computer Inc., Cupertino, CA).

Serious word processing requires a more expensive system than those mentioned above. The less expensive include an Atari 800™ with disk drive and printer (around $1,500) or a KayPro II with printer ($2,000 to $3,000). *The Atari Word Processor* is a helpful program that runs on the former. *Perfect Writer*™, an excellent package, is given free to purchasers of KayPro II.

WordStar® (MicroPro, San Rafael, CA) is referred to by some as the "Cadillac" of word processors (statements like this are bound to be temporary, since newer, more powerful packages are continually being produced). *WordStar* is given free to Osborne I™ purchasers. The trouble is, the Osborne screen is tiny—about 5 inches diagonally.

The IBM PC is an excellent computer for word processing. It's not cheap, however. After you've bought the disk drives, the printer, and the software, you've spent $3,000 or more for your system. Three recommended word processing programs for the IBM PC are *WordStar*, *Volkswriter*™—*Version 1.1* (Lifetree Software, Monterey, CA), and *Easy Writer II*™ (Information Unlimited Software, Sausalito, CA).

In Section II, I evaluate the computers you're likely to be interested in from several standpoints, one of which is how well they process words. For now, let me summarize:

Timex, Atari 400	Glum
VIC 20, Coco, and 99/4A	Less glum
Commodore 64™	Not bad
Atari 800, Apple IIe™	Acceptable
IBM PC and KayPro II	Good

Shop around. Mail-order discount houses offer word processing software at well below list price (obviously, be sure to deal with large, established vendors). Here are some examples:

WORD PROCESSING PROGRAM	LIST PRICE	ADVERTISED PRICE
WordStar	$495	$279
Perfect Writer	495	239
Easy Writer II	350	269

Mail-order shopping for word processing software is not recommended unless you've tested the program in advance. This is essential to make sure that you're comfortable using it and that it does what you want it to.

The most complete write-up I've seen comparing word processors is in a magazine called *Interface Age* (December 1982). The article is entitled "Buyer's Guide to Word Processing Software." It evaluates no less than 50 packages, using 36 different criteria. There are tables and tables of comparative information, and compatible hardware for each. In my view, this article is must reading for the Ultimately Rational Consumer.

Related Programs That Are Helpful

Spelling-check programs are offered by more and more companies that have word processing programs.

Writers who have trouble spelling will find these very helpful. Writers who spell well won't, although spelling checkers are helpful in finding certain kinds of typos (such as "teh," "adn," and others that are not words). Typos will still crop up when a legitimate word is inadvertently formed (such as when you meant to write "change," but typed "charge"; spelling checkers are no help here).

The spelling-check programs include a "dictionary" of thousands of words. The program reviews the writing, word by word, and checks to see if each word is in its dictionary. Only the lightning-fast processing of computers makes this practical. Some programs can check fifteen pages of text in a minute or so.

The words that aren't found in the dictionary are noted. As you examine each of these words, you are generally provided several choices:

1. You can leave it in (the word might be a proper name or a legitimate word that's not in the computer's dictionary).

2. You can replace it (type in "the" for "teh").

3. You can leave the word in and also have the computer add it to its dictionary, so the program will know it's OK in the future.

Some programs (such as *The WORD* and *The WORD PLUS*, Oasis Systems, San Diego, CA) even print words you might have meant. For example, if you hit "teh," the program might suggest "the." If "the" is what you want, a quick hit on the keyboard will make the substitution.

Grammar-check programs are also available. They check your grammar and word usage. A popular one, and reasonably priced at $50 to $149 (depending on your computer), is *Grammatik*™ (Aspen Software, Tijeras, NM). Built into the program is a list of weak or erroneous words or phrases. *Grammatik* searches your text. When it finds "weaknesses," it makes suggestions.

For example, if you write "ain't," *Grammatik* will tell you the word is "informal," and suggest you "revise." If you type "very," you are told you're using a "vague adverb" and are advised to "avoid or revise."

If you type "hopefully," it is suggested that you may have misused the word. (Did you know it's wrong to say: "Hopefully, they'll develop a faster dictionary program"? It's OK, however, to say: "The frog looked at the approaching princess hopefully.")

Grammatik provides some revealing statistics about your writing. For each piece it examines, it prints:

—the average number of words per sentence,

—the average number of letters per word,

—the number of questions and imperative statements,

—how many "short" sentences there are—i.e., those with less than fourteen words,

—the number of "long" sentences (over thirty words),

—how many forms of the verb "to be" were used (the fewer the better, I'm told), and

—how many prepositions were used.

Spelling and grammar programs serve another useful function. They teach. After being reminded over and over again that "mispelling" is misspelled, we begin putting in the other *s*. After being continually told that "seldom ever" is redundant, we seldom use it again.

Mail-merge programs are useful for sending form letters. The same letter can be sent to many people; the program automatically changes names and addresses. Some programs print mailing labels (on special forms that fit into printers) for those who, like me, detest addressing envelopes.

You can even "repersonalize" letters. Say you begin a letter, "It seems that whenever we're together, Debby, something unique and wonderful happens." Using mail-merge programs, we can change "Debby" to Pam and Diane and Kathy and...

People may catch on to this trick, however. Whenever I'm addressed by name in the text of a letter, the first thing I think is "form letter." On the other hand, mail-merging may become so prevalent someday that it will not be considered to be improperly impersonal.

Chapter 3

Education:
Learning, for Children and Adults

When I started researching this portion of the book, I had a skeptical attitude. I'd seen earlier computer learning aids that were basically electronic flashcards. For example, a problem would flash on the screen such as:

$$2 + 2 = ?$$

ENTER CORRECT ANSWER.

Big deal! Who needs a computer for this? A pencil, some cardboard, and a pair of scissors could accomplish the same thing—and for much less money.

Happily, educational software is improving at a rapid rate. And newer learning techniques are being employed to take advantage of the unique ability of the computer to teach. Let's look at how the computer surpasses flashcards or textbooks in teaching:

1. More than books, computers can make learning enjoyable. They can disguise the fact that the student is learning by masquerading the teaching in the form of a game. Thus students can pop balloons as they enter numerical answers to problems; other programs combine teaching with pinball games, space shootouts, or happy walks through colorful forests. The student plays and enjoys the game, learning almost inadvertently.

2. Computers can interact with the students, that

is, respond specifically to their answers. This is well beyond the realm of textbooks. If the student gives a correct answer, the computer can uniquely praise the student by playing a humorous tune or showing a colorful graphic. If the student answers incorrectly, he is assisted in trying to find the correct answer by being given clues and words of encouragement.

3. Computers can evaluate student performance. The rapid computational ability of computers can be used to provide "grades" instantaneously and accurately (a dramatic example is a program that gives you words per minute in a typing drill *as* you are typing). The computer can also provide comments such as "100% right! That was great, John!" or "Kathy, you can do better. Why not try it again?"

4. Computers do motivate us to practice (some say this applies even more to children because of their familiarity with the TV screen). For example, in reviewing educational software I found myself reluctant to stop playing some of the programs—even the ones that "taught" me things I already knew. To show you how hooked I became, while preparing this book I was typing probably eight to ten hours a day. Yet when reviewing one typing program, I stayed with it far longer than necessary to review it. I continued "practicing" typing solely because I wanted to continue the game. Talk about a busman's holiday!

Now let's talk about what subjects are covered by computer programs. There are literally thousands of educational programs available covering a hundred or more subjects.

You can learn arithmetic, spelling, typing, physics, chemistry, geometry, or algebra. You can learn how to read faster, prepare for SAT tests, recognize different types of dinosaurs (I hope you never have to apply this skill), or perform chem lab or ecology sim-

ulations. You can learn techniques in predicting vol-
cano eruptions, understand how to read maps, fly an
airplane, identify aircraft, and learn about U.S. pres-
idents. You can drill in any of a dozen languages,
including Japanese and Russian.

That's the good news. The bad news is that the
quality of educational software varies widely. Some of
the programs are just about worthless; others are gems.
And many fall between these two extremes.

What I'm going to do now is review a representative
sample of some of the programs. This should serve
several purposes:

1. Show you *how* the programs teach. You've read
that computers can teach all kinds of things; but you'd
like to know what they do to teach—specifically.

2. Give you an idea of what to look for in good
programs and in poor ones.

3. To a limited degree, you may be helped in actually purchasing software. This section isn't meant
to be a buying guide; the field is far too broad for
that and, indeed, better software is coming out all the
time (Chapter 9 recommends how to find good software). However, you may spot a program or two that
strike your fancy, and for this reason I include the
name of the manufacturer of each program discussed.

Now I'll describe some of the software that instructs
in a variety of subjects.

Preschool Learning

Learning Nursery Rhymes

Programs allow you to sing nursery rhymes with
your children. You read the words from the screen,

the child looks at colorful nursery-rhyme characters, and the computer plays the melody. One software package has nine nursery rhymes and three simple video games. In one game, Mary collects three little lambs, with you-know-what played during the process. (*Micro Mother Goose*™, by Software Productions, Columbus, Ohio; for ages 3 to 9; overall rating B.)

Learning the Alphabet

Programs help children learn the alphabet using various techniques. One is to have the child move a cursor in a colorful maze, selecting the twenty-six letters in the correct sequence. It gets the job done, converting learning the alphabet into an arcade maze game. But in my view, alphabet learning programs have one severe limitation. Once the alphabet's learned, I would think the child would get bored, and the disk would sit in a closet gathering dust. (*BOP-A-BET*™, by Sunnyside Soft, Fresno, CA; overall rating D+.)

Learning to Count

Various objects are shown on the screen—balloons, faces, balls, and so on. The child must count them and enter the correct number; simple addition problems, with supporting graphics, are included as well. The color and graphics of the computer are used effectively to maintain children's interest. (*Counting Bee*, by Edu-Ware Services, Agoura, CA; overall rating B.)

Memorization and the Use of the Computer

One preschool program, *Facemaker*, incorporates several "games," which combine fun and learning for the child:

1. The child constructs faces, choosing several different (and often entertaining) mouths, eyes, ears, noses and hairstyles.

2. The child may make the face wink, cry, smile, frown, wiggle its ears, or stick out its tongue.

3. The child may write a little "program," entering a sequence of facial expressions.

4. The child may play a form of Simple Simon. (The computer causes the face to make a series of expressions, starting with one expression, and adding one more with each repetition.) The child tries to duplicate what the computer has done. He's rewarded or gently chided, depending upon his performance. (*Facemaker*, by Spinnaker, Cambridge, MA; overall rating B.)

More Advanced Learning

Learning Arithmetic

Programs combine arcade games and math drills. For example, *Multiploy*™ (Reston Software, Reston, VA; overall rating C) has a space-invaders-type game. Aliens of various shapes, with arithmetic problems printed on their surface, descend from the top of the screen. The student must type in the correct answer to destroy the aliens. Otherwise he is zapped—just as in the arcades.

Multiploy has problems in all four arithmetic functions, with three different skill levels. The game loses some of its arcade appeal because of the delays in typing in the numbers, and hence shooting the aliens. But it *is* one way to get kids to do their math drills.

Another math program is *Elementary Math*™, (by Muse Software; overall rating C). The student is presented a series of problems in the four arithmetic functions. The program uses the color and sounds of the computer to keep the student interested. What distinguishes this package from simple electronic flash cards is that the student is given help if he makes errors. At the end of each drill, the computer grades the student and suggests which drill should be tried next. This program loses effectiveness because of its slow response time; furthermore, the colors tend to run together, making the information difficult to read.

Learning Word Skills

In one game, the player is given a list of ten words that are parts of compound words (e.g., "flash" and "light," making up "flashlight"). The computer is given an eleven-word list (we don't know what it is). Separate turns are taken with the computer creating compound words from the words on the list. The first one to run out of words wins. This is a simple game, but it effectively teaches spelling and vocabulary. It's recommended for grades 3 through 6. It's an engaging game and has a high learn/fun factor. (*Wordmate*™, by T.H.E.S.I.S., Garden City, MI; overall rating B.)

Computer word games teach word skills with varying degrees of success. One has the student fill letters into a 5-by-5 table, creating as many three-, four-, and five-letter words as possible. The player is awarded points, depending on the difficulty in placing various letters of the alphabet. The game is of only average interest; it may assist in learning words, but basically it's an expensive form of electronic alphabet solitaire. (*Pandemonium*™, by Soft Images, Mahwah, NJ; overall rating C−.)

Learning Fractions and Prime Numbers

Computers can be used effectively to provide interesting instruction by capitalizing on the graphics, color, and sound. The student is then asked questions about the material covered, and his answers are evaluated. If the student is incorrect, he is given guidance in reaching the correct answer.

A program that does this effectively in teaching fractions is *EDU-WARE Fractions*™ (Edu-Ware Services, Agoura, CA; overall rating A−). The program teaches how to find common denominators and how to add, subtract, multiply, and divide fractions. When the student feels ready, he is administered tests in each of the areas.

Another helpful package is *Fractions—Basic Concepts* (Sterling Swift, Los Angeles, CA; overall rating B). The lessons are personalized; that is, the student types in his first name and is continually referred to by name. Sterling Swift also produces lessons on the four basic arithmetic functions, one disk per function, in either English or Spanish. The programs are excellent, are easy to follow, and provide extensive interaction between student and computer.

Learning X-Y Coordinates

One software package lets students learn the concept of positive and negative numbers and X-Y coordinates. A series of five games is presented, each of varying difficulty. In the simplest, the child merely tries to bracket a number from −3 to +3 on a continuum and then guess the number.

In another game, the computer draws a picture on an X-Y grid of 100 squares (from −10 to +10). The picture is formed by a sequence of dots on the screen. The student types in the coordinates of the dots until the picture is completed.

I almost hate to admit how much time I spent playing the final game (called *Roadblock*™); these games are for kids, right? The object is to entrap a bank robber (actually a moving cursor) by moving roadblocks around the grid. There's a time limit, so the quick and accurate identifications of X-Y coordinates (from −5 to +5) is essential. After a few games, you'll be able to read grid numbers as well as any air traffic controller. (*Bumble Plot*™, for ages 8 to 13, by The Learning Company®, Portola Valley, CA; overall rating A.) The package comes with an attractive, colorful instruction book and a set of "activity cards" to play other grid games.

Learning to Type

A number of programs are available to teach the basic skills of typing. One effective package combines typing lessons with a space-invaders-type game. The easiest lessons require typing letters on the "home row" (the a,s,d,f,g,h,j,k, and l). Harder lessons include typing eight-letter words, numbers, punctuation marks, and the less common symbols.

At the end of each lesson, the student is shown a score, his average speed (in words per minute), the number of words typed, and the number of mistakes.

The program is limited in the number of letters,

words, and symbols. While it can't be construed as a thorough typing course, its strong point is that most students will find it difficult to stop "playing." (*Master Type*™, by Lightning Software, Palo Alto, CA; overall rating B.)

Other typing programs are not as much fun, but are more instructive and of greater benefit to the serious student. For example, *Typing Tutor II*™ (Microsoft, Bellevue, WA; overall rating A−) consists of a series of drills, storing information for up to 49 different students. The user may practice letters and numbers (new keys are gradually introduced), type practice paragraphs, or, at the end of each lesson, take a typing test. The program allows the student to concentrate on weaknesses (such as typing numbers).

Here again, the student's progress is monitored, and he is informed of his speed, number of errors, and even which keys are struck in error. The exercises are rigorous. If the student persists, there's no question that he'll learn to type well.

Learning to Sight-Read Music

One program teaches the student to read music and to train his ear to hear music as well. A phrase of music is displayed on the screen. The computer then plays the phrase, but with one of the notes incorrectly sounded. The student must guess which is the incorrect note.

The answer is graded. Then the computer prints the musical notation for what was actually played. If desired, the student may instruct the program to play the phrase correctly.

The user tells the computer the maximum number of sharps or flats to be included in the exercises. Thus, beginning music students may start by reading in the basic key of C major and gradually progress to more difficult keys.

Reading an English Micrometer

A micrometer is an instrument that measures objects with great accuracy, providing readings to the nearest thousandth of an inch. The program gives the student instruction in the values of the numerical graduations on the barrel and sleeve of a micrometer. A replica of the micrometer is displayed on the screen. A series of objects is shown, and the student is asked to type in the correct readings from a visual observation of the markings on the barrel and sleeve. (No title, by Minnesota Educational Computer Consortium, a state educational organization; overall rating B.)

Learning Weights and Measures

The student is asked a series of questions on weights and measures. One example is "How many quarts in a gallon?" The computer graphics are then put into play, as we see a gallon of milk poured into four quart containers. This is an effective way to teach. The student is far more likely to recall the visual representation than to memorize the dry statement "There are four quarts in a gallon." (No title, Minnesota Educational Computer Consortium; overall rating A.)

General Chemistry

One package (*Programs for Learning*™, New Milford, CT; overall rating B) does a competent job of covering chemical subjects and makes effective use of computer graphics (for example, a diagram of a pH meter with appropriate readings is shown). The package has excellent documentation.

Flora and Fauna

One program called *Odell Lake* (Minnesota Educational Consortium) provides for the student to choose one of six types of fish: whitefish, chub, etc. He is then shown a picture of a lake, with a boy fishing at one end. The fish selected by the student is portrayed on the screen and encounters other fish and birds. The student must decide whether to eat the other fish, escape, ignore it, or select one of several other options. After so doing, he is informed whether he made the correct choice. Most students, after playing several games, will learn which fish eat other fish, which ignore each other, and so on. *Odell Lake* would no doubt be of interest to naturalists. City boy that I am, I had no idea that a Mackinaw trout is such a voracious and dangerous creature.

Learning About Relationships

Lovers or Strangers™ is a unique program that helps to evaluate the nature of a relationship between two people. While the program could be used as a party game, the accompanying write-up gives a realistic evaluation of relationships and refers to the program as "a computer game with a serious side."

Both parties respond to a series of questions and guess how the other party would answer each question. The computer evaluates the responses and rates the two parties (on a continuum from 1 to 100) as perfect opposites or a perfect match, from seven standpoints: communication, love and romance, values, sex, work and money, spirituality, and play. The program was designed by two psychotherapists. (*Lovers or Strangers*, Alpine Software, Colorado Springs, CO; overall rating B.)

Learning About Yourself

Programs are available that allow us to take a series of tests and evaluate ourselves from various standpoints. One, called *Understand Yourself*™, has nine tests. Included are tests in assertiveness, conscience, marital adjustment, scale of values, personal adjustment, and sexual attitudes.

This program is similar to the reader tests often published in magazines. The user types in the answers, adds up his score, and discovers how he did by reading the computer evaluation printed on the screen. I presume that the analyses provided by *Understand Yourself* are valid; the author has credentials in the field. Nevertheless, the evaluations are cryptic and superficial. It seems to me that magazine quizzes are as effective as this program, although the computer does the tabulating for the reader. (*Understand Yourself*, Huntington Computing, Corcor, CA; overall rating C −).

Learning Algebra

Algebra 1 (Edu-Ware Services, Agoura, Ca; overall rating A −) provides a detailed course in algebra. The programs are contained on five diskettes; algebraic definitions, rules, examples, sample problems, and tests are included.

Learning Languages

The Russian Disk™ (Instant Software, Peterborough, NH; overall rating B) teaches Russian vowels, consonants, and commonly used words for food, drink, types of places to eat, and street signs. The program is intended to assist potential travelers to Russia who want to "get by"; it's not for those who want an in-depth knowledge of the Russian language.

The screen displays various words in both English and Russian and drills the student on comprehension. The program is helpful in how it anticipates situations that might be encountered. For example, the word "smoking" is displayed in Russian. Then two signs are shown, one saying "No smoking" and the second "Smoking prohibited." *The Russian Disk* is definitely of value to the traveler who wants to stay out of a Communist detention cell for some minor infraction.

Similar programs are available for other languages, including French, Spanish, German, and Italian.

Additional Word Skills

Numerous programs familiarize students with words by presenting anagram drills. The most common type displays letters in a word out of sequence. The student must type in the proper word.

One package that attempts this in a poor way is *Word Scrambler and Super Speller*™ (Avant-Garde Creations, Eugene, OR; overall rating D−). Anagrams are shown. In an unimaginative drill without graphics, the screen simply displays a scrambled word; the student must try to unscramble it. Worse yet, there were several instances in which I could not continue the exercise because of apparent programming bugs. This package is definitely not recommended.

A more effective program of this type is *Magic Spells*™ (Advanced Learning Technology, Portola Valley, CA; overall rating B−). An 11-year-old girl created the excellent graphics for this program. The student is presented with a series of anagrams. If he guesses wrong, he is given help by the program (the correctly positioned letters are displayed). There is an imaginative reward-point system to provide motivation for the student to do well.

Caution

Some software is as dry and boring as the most ponderous of texts.

One not inexpensive package of education programs teaches punctuation, math, and science. The science program is pure text and is so dry that I doubt many students would voluntarily spend much time using it. The punctuation lessons add a few graphics, but the material is also presented in a boring way. A lesson in solving equations is similarly bland. Despite these deficiencies, the programs cost $40 to $50 per diskette. (*How to Read in the Content Areas* and *Punctuation I and II*, by Educational Activities, Inc., Freeport, NY; overall rating: D.)

To repeat, there are some really poor programs on the market. Don't buy software based on impressive advertising copy or because it comes in a pretty box. In Chapter 9, I discuss how to make sure you get what you pay for when purchasing software.

Chapter 4

Financial Spreadsheets: Home Electronic Accounting

When business hardware/software packages are merchandised, the software invariably includes two types of programs. One is a word processor; the second is an "electronic spreadsheet" or "calc-type" program (I will call them "calcs" from now on).

First, let me tell you a little success story. A young fellow growing up in Philadelphia became interested in computers. Being quite intelligent, he ended up going to MIT. Then he enrolled in Harvard Business School.

One day, he was sitting in a finance class when the professor had a complex "spreadsheet" (table of numbers) on the blackboard. Someone in the class would suggest that perhaps sales wouldn't go up so much or that maybe cost-of-goods-sold would be lower or that interest expense might be underestimated. Whenever anyone suggested an alternative, the spreadsheet had to be calculated all over again, with erasers and chalk dust flying. Of course, the students had hand-held calculators at their disposal, but in working with a string of numbers, just one mispunched digit and it was back to ground zero.

The student, now 27, was Daniel Bricklin. He felt frustrated (I sympathize with him—I took the same course). But Bricklin did something about it. He ingeniously put together a computer program to do all these calculations "automatically."

The program worked at Harvard Business School. Word spread, and the program started working in a few businesses. Then a few more businesses. The program came to be called *VisiCalc*®, which stands for "visible calculator." It sold and sold, until, 400,000 copies later, it became known as the program so good it's worth buying a computer for. People literally ran out and bought Apple® computers so they could run *VisiCalc*—and the program wasn't cheap, at around $200 a copy. Imagine. Thousands of people bought $2,000 to $3,000 computers so they could run Daniel's program. (Bricklin is now an older fella, 31, and he runs his $7 million company, Software Arts, in Wellesley, MA.)

Others quickly recognized the value of *VisiCalc* and realized that it could be used in home financial calculations, too. Calcs are now available for the Atari®, VIC 20™, and other home computers—even the tiny Timex 1000™.

Calcs are referred to as "electronic spreadsheet" programs because that's exactly what they create—a computerized table with numbers on it. Most allow letters of the alphabet to be posted, too. This is necessary to create column and row headings (e.g., "income," "auto expense," "interest income," "January," "1983," etc.).

How might a calc help you? Let's look at an example. Say you're one of the few Americans who faithfully keeps a budget (I've only met one person who does).

You're in your den on a Friday night, with a huge accounting sheet in front of you (you know, the kind with all the predrawn columns and rows). While thinking about the boys drinking down at the lodge, you're quite proud of your self-discipline, as you laboriously "post" (an accounting term) your income, your wife's

Household Budget — 1983

Income	JAN.	FEB.	MARCH	APRIL	MAY	JUNE	JULY	AUG.	SEPT.	OCT.	NOV.	DEC.	YEAR 1983
My income	$	$	$	$	$	$	$	$	$	$	$	$	$
Wife's income	$	$	$	$	$	$	$	$	$	$	$	$	$
B of A savings	$	$	$	$	$	$	$	$	$	$	$	$	$
UCB savings	$	$	$	$	$	$	$	$	$	$	$	$	$
AT&T dividends	$	$	$	$	$	$	$	$	$	$	$	$	$
Warner dividends	$	$	$	$	$	$	$	$	$	$	$	$	$
IBM dividends	$	$	$	$	$	$	$	$	$	$	$	$	$
Warner-Lambert dividends	$	$	$	$	$	$	$	$	$	$	$	$	$
Rent from summer house	$	$	$	$	$	$	$	$	$	$	$	$	$
Total Income	$	$	$	$	$	$	$	$	$	$	$	$	$38,638

Note: Dollar amounts would be posted to the spaces on this spreadsheet. I've filled in only the total income for the year ($38,638). The expense spreadsheet would look even more formidable, having (in our example) twenty-eight line items instead of the nine shown here.

part-time income, interest from a couple of savings accounts, four dividend payments from various stocks you own, and a rent or two. You write all figures in by month, for the coming year. Then you add the column and row totals, until the spreadsheet looks something like the example shown here.

Now it's time to do the expenses. This task is not nearly as easy. You've got rent, food, auto payments, clothing, five different kinds of insurance, utilities, six types of taxes, and so on. You post all these items as well as your oldest child's tuition payments, which come due at the end of every quarter.

Then you remember the gift category. You put in those amounts (three birthdays—in January, May, and August—and a slug of money in December for Christmas). When you're finished, you end up with 28 expense categories.

Now you add up all the rows and columns. You test your accuracy by "cross-footing" (another accounting term) the totals to get the grand total for the year. The expenses don't balance. The columns (monthly totals) add to $37,693. The rows (expense category totals) add to $35,649. (You hope the rows are right.)

You add the numbers again and again and again. Fifty minutes later, you've got the expense budget balanced. (Actually neither original total was right; the actual amount is $36,433).

It's now 3:00 A.M. So you go to bed. The next day, Saturday, you dutifully ignore *Wide World of Sports* and return to the den. You put the whole spreadsheet together, comparing total income and expense. Things are looking good; you'll have an extra $2,205 for the year. You put in savings and investment rows to take up the slack.

Your wife comes into the room.

"Dear," she says, "do you need anything? Got to pick up Debby at dancing class."

You nod back, almost not hearing. Then something clicks. Dancing class? *Dancing class?* My God! We pay $45 a month for Debby's ballet lessons! How could I have forgotten?

You take eraser and pencil and spend another hour and a half figuring the budget all over again.

Just as you finish, son Doug comes in and announces that he wants to go to computer camp this summer. It's $300, but he'll learn all about computer programming. You feel that he should go. After all, these days a kid's got to know about computers. So you tell Doug he can go to camp. But not before taking the budget spreadsheet and ripping it to shreds.

You think, "What the hell. We'll get through the year. We always have."

As I mentioned in Chapter 1, most home computers have budget programs that can handle home budgeting, as can calc programs. But I've given this example because it will help you to understand the types of problems for which calcs are the most useful. Once a user sets up his spreadsheet (computer people like to call this a "model"), he's basically done. If any number or set of numbers changes, the rest of the spreadsheet automatically recalculates itself.

If you need to put in dancing school or computer camp, if you get an unexpected raise, if your house insurance goes up, or if anything else changes, you simply type in the new figure on the keyboard. Before you can blink, the revised spreadsheet is displayed before you—with total accuracy.

There are a variety of uses for calcs in the home. Picture as well how calcs can help businesses. Managers have to cope with changing interest rates, new orders, bad debts, additional employees, changes in payroll tax rates...the list is endless. Now it becomes clear why Bricklin's *VisiCalc* sold so many computers.

Imagine the Big Boss saying to his financial VP, "What if sales go up eight percent over last year? How would we do?"

An hour later, he returns in a more optimistic mood, and says, "I'm feeling better about this year's prospects. What if sales go up twelve percent?"

This is why the ads say that the calc programs solve "what-if" questions.

"Fine and good," you say. "But I don't own a business and I don't keep a budget. How does this affect me?"

Good question. It may not. This is one of the areas where home computer programs may be perilously close to being a solution in search of a problem. If you're the type of person who methodically keeps track of things, you may find a good use for a calc. If you're not, forget it.

Or perhaps you're like me and keep saying, "Someday I'll set it all up. But not just now." Maybe the purchase of a computer and a calc program will give you the motivation to set up a budget. On the other hand, maybe you'll tire of the whole thing after two months (just to be safe, you might consider buying a computer with a good space-invaders-type game).

There's a way for you to see how a calc works, firsthand, if there's a Radio Shack® Computer Center in your town. The best demonstration I've seen of what a calc can do is on a disk that Radio Shack has prepared for its TRS-80® computers. When put in "demo mode" (another computer term), the program steps you through an example on the screen (instead of income and expenses, it uses sales, costs, and profits). You just sit and watch. As soon as you see the computer instantaneously recalculate the many numbers in the "matrix" (a fancy word for "table"), you'll immediately realize how helpful calcs can be.

Calcs can be used for any type of problem for which a spreadsheet is needed. It could be a listing of how much rent you'll get each month from your fourteen properties (if you're so lucky). Or maybe you want to compile the value of your stock-market investments, bonds, and savings accounts and see how they'll accumulate over the years, given various assumptions about interest rates and changes in the Dow Jones Index.

Or maybe you want to construct a long-term budget, putting in your annual income and your expenses for the next ten years, assuming different levels of inflation. In experimenting with one calc, I put the current cost of some products in the first column, including a quart of milk, loaf of bread, bottle of scotch, television set, automobile, and house. I told the computer to calculate how much each of these items would cost, for each of the next thirty years, assuming a 10 percent rate of inflation. The calculations were made in seconds and posted to the table. (I hate to tell you this, but an $8,000 car will cost over $139,000 in thirty years at that rate of inflation.)

Some Calc Programs

Spreadsheets are usually described by how many columns and rows they permit. For example, *VisiCalc* allows 63 columns and 254 lines. You obviously don't see all the information at one time on the screen. The screen "scrolls"—that is, it pans across the sheet so you see whatever part of the table you want. (Actually the columns and rows change instantaneously, so it's not technically a scroll; let's call it a "jerky scroll.") Some calcs allow you to split the screen so, for example, you can see lines 1 through 6 and lines 145 through 151 simultaneously.

Here is a description of several of the many calcs that are on the market.

Tiny Plan ™

The cheapest calc I know of—in fact, it's nearly free—is called *Tiny Plan*™. It can be run on the VIC 20, Coco, Atari, or Apple computers. The program listing is printed in a magazine (*Compute!*, December 1982). Entering the program is a laborious and error-prone task. The listing contains about 250 instructions; a typical one looks like this:

```
INPUTR$:IFR() " "THENCN(I) = LEFT$(R$ + BL$,10)
```

Tiny Plan is limited mathematically. It can handle the four arithmetic functions and several percentage calculations. It adds up column and row totals, even if you don't want them, and allows for the display of only ten numbers at one time.

But what do you want for nothing (or for $2.50, if you bought the magazine)?

Timex Vu-Calc ™

A calc put out by Timex for its 1000 computer is called *Vu-Calc* and costs about $20. *Vu-Calc* provides 36 columns (numbered from 01 to 36) and 26 rows (labeled A through Z). At any given time, 27 boxes are displayed on the screen, 3 columns by 9 rows.

A cursor indicates which box (called "cell") is currently being worked with. The cursor is moved by one of the four arrows on the computer keyboard. The screen jerky-scrolls in any of the four directions, as directed by the movement of the cursor.

The user can store date in any of the boxes and generate other data by putting in formulas for any of the boxes. For example, if the number 15 is entered into box A01, and the number 35 in Box A02, the user may, for box A03, put in the value "A01 + A02." The computer then calculates the value for box A03, which, of course, is 50. Whenever the user changes the value in A01 or A02, box A03 is automatically recalculated.

Up to 40 formulas may be entered (for any 40 boxes). Each formula may contain up to 32 characters. The formulas may include addition (indicated by +), subtraction (−), multiplication (*), division (/), and the use of exponents (**). You may refer to any of the boxes in the formulas, from A01 to Z36. You are also allowed to "chain" the formulas, so a series of values can be computed and posted to the table. Thus the user can instruct the computer to calculate annual compound interest for each of 30 years with a single command.

Other Calcs

Commodore produces a program called *Simplicalc*™ for the VIC 20. This program, which contains the basic characteristics of a calc, requires the use of either a cassette recorder or a disk drive in order to store data. Naturally, the user will need a printer if a paper copy of the spreadsheet is desired.

The Texas Instruments spreadsheet program for the TI 99/4A™ is called *Microsoft® Multiplan*™. It requires a disk drive and a 32K memory expansion unit.

For the Atari, Apple, and IBM Personal Computer®, the original calc, *VisiCalc*, is available, from VisiCorp®. As mentioned, both versions provide for 66 columns and 254 lines. The user navigates about the table using the cursor. Four columns of 20 lines each may be viewed simultaneously under "normal" use. This can be changed, however. If the width of the columns is shrunk, more columns can be viewed; if column width is expanded, fewer may be viewed at one time.

One excellent feature of *VisiCalc* is that the formula for the box at which the cursor is located is always displayed at the top of the screen. *VisiCalc* currently lists for $250; I've seen it on sale for as low as $184.

Calc Help

I know that this sounds like a truism, but it is true that the uses you'll find for a calc program are limited only by your imagination. If your imagination needs a little stimulation, help is available.

There are books that contain uses for calc programs. One of the better is called *VisiCalc Home and Office Companion* (Osborne/McGraw-Hill Books, $16). This book describes fifty possible uses for *VisiCalc* (which apply to most other calcs as well). The uses are categorized into seven areas, two of which apply to home use: personal finance and household aids.

Computer magazine articles often contain uses for calcs. For example, an article in *Creative Computing*, February 1983, explains how we can use a calc to analyze an IRA (Individual Retirement Account). The program calculates when the investor should take the money and run; that is, when early withdrawal penalties are overcome by tax savings and interest earned.

A use of *VisiCalc* for those who have real estate

investments was published in *Desktop Computing*, January 1983. The article explains how a calc program can be set up to determine the effect on cash flow when investment property is purchased, taking into account financing costs, finance points paid, annual debt service, and a host of other factors.

There is even a service available which helps to select the best calc for your needs from among fifty-seven electronic spreadsheet programs. And the ads claim that it's free (ITM Software Division, Lafayette, CA; 800-334-3404).

Mega-Calcs

Nothing seems to stay the same in the computer field. This is certainly true of the calc programs.

Programs are available that improve on *VisiCalc*. I'll give odds that Bricklin and company will be coming out with newer versions as well (there have been several revisions already). *Multiplan** (Microsoft, Bellevue, MA), already mentioned, allows the user to assign names to individual spreadsheet boxes. Thus instead of having to type in formulas such as "A03 − B03 = C03" you can enter "Profit = Income − Expense."

Software houses are developing calcs to allow the linking of spreadsheets, so users may transfer data from one table to another. Others permit the combining of spreadsheets, so quarterly spreadsheets can be added together to derive annual tables, and regional forecasts can be accumulated into overall company projections.

There's no doubt that many computerphiles from

---

*An excellent program which received *InfoWorld*'s award for best software package of 1982.

coast to coast are staying up at night trying to emulate Daniel Bricklin by devising some kind of Super-Duper-Calc. And I have a feeling some will succeed.

One Final Word

Some of you have an obvious need for a calc program. Others may get some use out of such a program, but must first think a little bit about how. Yet others will need a calc about as much as an extra mortgage payment.

My advice: Don't buy a calc program unless you know *exactly* what you plan to do with it and how you can specifically benefit.

Chapter 5

Information: Bringing a Storehouse of Information into the Home

Home computers can provide you access to information on just about any subject under the sun. In many cases, the information is more up-to-date than data that you'd get from any other source.

There are companies that have huge computers (called "mainframes") that maintain enormous masses of information (called "data bases"). Some of this information, such as news reports and stock quotations, is updated minute by minute. Just about any home computer can tie you into these data bases. You must get a "modem" (we defined this earlier—a device that allows your computer to be connected, via your telephone, to another computer). You also need a software package (they are given fancy names like "terminal emulator program" and "asynchronous communication software") that lets your computer tie into the data base.

You pay a one-time fee to join most information services plus an hourly service charge. You do *not* get socked for long-distance charges, however. You hook up either by dialing a local number or using a toll-free number.

These purveyors of information refer to themselves by such names as "consumer data base network" or "interactive videotex service." I'll call them "info companies."

Info companies can provide us with information that can be valuable because things change so rapidly. To wit:

1. New York, American, Pacific, and Midwest stock quotations (with a minimum 15-minute delay, which the exchanges insist on)

2. Prices of corporate bonds, stock options, over-the-counter stocks, and mutual fund shares

3. Current airline schedules and rates, both of which change frequently

4. Up-to-the-minute news

You might wonder why people would pay to get news, when all they have to do is turn on the radio or TV. One reason is that with the info services, you can request news in specific areas, such as news about Japan, the U.S. Supreme Court, business executive changes, the Internal Revenue Service, or the casino and gaming industry.

The info services offer another advantage. Have you ever tried to get a copy of yesterday's paper? Or worse yet, one that's three or four days old? The info companies provide this "old news." For example, the Dow Jones info service provides access to news files going back 90 days.

Information that doesn't change quickly can be worth having, simply because you get the data exactly when you want it. For example, if you want reviews of movies, restaurants, or books, you don't have to search out last Sunday's *Los Angeles Times* or this week's *New Yorker*, only to find that the item you're interested in isn't there. For that matter, you can even read the *Los Angeles Times*, the *New York Times*, or the *Washington Post*. Or you can get the UPI and AP newswires.

You can send "mail" to other users of the service. Some services have a "broadcast" feature that allows you to send mail to a hundred or more users. This is a mixed blessing; the Era of Electronic Junk Mail may be rapidly approaching.

Résumés may be left on an "electronic bulletin board" for employer-members. Or ads for selling or swapping items may be posted (and you get the instant gratification of knowing the ad's listed *now*). You can even buy things and order airline tickets (usually a credit-card number is required).

Users can get dates by posting notices on the bulletin board, such as "Sincere, young computer hacker, no drinking, smoking, or drugs, with an interest in chem-lab simulations, desires exciting, vivacious, attractive blonde under 20, for exciting evenings discussing Avogadro's Number Experiment and Acid Base Titration."

The rates for many services appear low. The most popular service costs only $5 an hour. But, as with our phone bills, you may be amazed at the size of the statement at the end of the month. Once you've plugged into the system, it's tempting to stay there, wandering around through the data, seeing what's available, having "conversations" with other members from all over the country, and browsing through the want ads and personal messages. Some services allow you to query what charges you've run up, at any time.

How helpful are these services? It depends on you. When I first hooked into one, I was like a kid in a candy store. I even looked up airline schedules for cities I'd never been in (and hope never to have to go to) just out of curiosity. But then I'm a person who usually reads three or four newspapers a day, and I watch *Good Morning, America*, *Today*, and *The CBS Morning Show* simultaneously, obsessively clicking back and forth with the TV remote controller.

I suspect that most people will be intrigued and interested in the new information they can glean from the info services. If you like to read newspapers or *Time* magazine, or watch network news, chances are you'll find the info services interesting, and probably helpful. If you're the type that could spend hours looking through an encyclopedia, just finding out about things, you could easily get addicted.

Info services may not be of interest to those who don't read the paper or care to watch the news. Some people are happy with the information they now get and do not need or want any more (such as one of my ex-roommates, who reads *Playboy* and *Penthouse*— period). In other words, the value of info services (and just about any other service, for that matter) depends on your interests.

How useful are these services? This, too, depends on you. What information do you feel you need in order to succeed (or just survive)? If you must have up-to-date financial data, don't even consider *not* plugging into the Dow Jones Service. If you fly a lot and often put your airline itinerary together at the last minute—perhaps at 2:00 A.M. when the travel bureaus are closed—an info service will be helpful. If you're a lawyer, doctor, or farmer, and want to save time finding legal precedents, diagnoses of symptoms, or the price of hogs, you'll find the services useful.

CompuServe ™

CompuServe is the most popular information service, with over 40,000 users. Owners of just about any computer can hook up to CompuServe with a modem and a software package. The one-time registration fee is $20, and the package can be purchased at any Radio Shack. With membership, you get one free hour on

CompuServe (and also on the Dow Jones Service) and a subscription to CompuServe's user magazine, *Today*. The hourly charge is $5, and the user may hook into the service from 6:00 P.M. to 5:00 A.M. during the week, and at any time on weekends and holidays. Owners of the VIC 20® need not pay the initial fee.

If you want to use CompuServe during "prime time," that is, from 5:00 A.M. to 6:00 P.M. during working days, the charge is $22.50 per hour, with a two-hour-per-month minimum.

When you buy the package, you're given a sealed pack which contains your user identification number and "secret password." You're also given a user's guide, which is reasonably clear and complete.

When you dial up the service, you first see a "main menu." A menu in the world of computers is a list of the alternatives that you have—just like a menu in a restaurant. Instead of prices, though, you're usually told what key or keys to strike on the computer keyboard to "order" the desired item.

CompuServe's main menu looks like this:

1. Home Services
2. Business and Financial
3. Personal Computing
4. Services for Professionals
5. User Information
6. Index

You then press the appropriate numbered key to raise the category desired. Usually, you'll encounter another menu (CompuServe has over 900 different menus). You keep progressing along the menu choices until you zero in on the category that you want.

For example, if you press "6" for "Index" you'll see:

1. To search index
2. Complete Index List

When you strike "1" the screen message says,

Enter Keyword

This indicates that you should type in the subject in which you're interested. If, for example, you type in "games," you'll get a list that starts:

Adventure Games
Backgammon Games
Blackjack

and so on.

It's possible for the user to spend much time and money searching through menus. However, CompuServe provides a way to proceed directly to the "page" desired by typing in the page "number" (which actually consists of letters and numbers).

A massive amount of data is available to the user. Some of the more interesting items are:

1. 22 volumes of *The World Book Encyclopedia.*

2. A simulated Citizens Band (CB) radio network, which ties members across the country together "on channel." You "talk" to each other by typing messages on the keyboard. This is currently the most popular use of CompuServe.

3. A message system which allows you to send mail or read your mail.

4. A "What's New" category which lists new information that has become available. For example, if you select "What's New," the following may appear on the computer screen:

Income Tax Preparation
March Movie Reviews
Dallas, TX, User Notice
Computerthon Results
Today Newsletter

5. You can post messages on a "National Bulletin Board" which can be read by any user.

6. A "feedback" category which allows all members to make suggestions or register complaints to CompuServe (CompuServe, quite fairly, doesn't charge users for the elapsed time while using feedback).

The Source℠

The Source, owned by *Reader's Digest*, is CompuServe's main competitor, with about 30,000 subscribers. The sign-up charge is steeper, $100, for which you're given an account number, password, and user's manual. If you decide you don't like the service during the first 30 days, the $100 is refundable (less any charges that were run up). The user fee is $6 to $8 per hour ($21 during prime-time business hours). There's a minimum charge of $10 per month. A special service called Source*Plus℠, which provides business information, costs $10 to $15 per hour ($30 during prime time).

Source information is similar to that of CompuServe. It includes:

1. Airline schedules (users can make reservations through a travel organization and receive airline tickets in the mail)

2. The UPI newswire (business news, general news, sports)

3. Personal résumés and job openings

4. Electronic mail and a public bulletin board

5. A home medical adviser; you answer queries posed by the electronic doctor and get back information on various illnesses

6. Current and historical data on common stocks and abstracts from nearly thirty business publications (Source*Plus)

The Source main menu looks like this:

1. News and Reference Resources
2. Business and Financial Markets
3. Catalog Shopping
4. Home and Leisure
5. Education and Career
6. Mail and Communications
7. Creating and Computing
8. Source*Plus

Dow Jones Information Service

The Dow Jones Service, owned by the company that publishes the *Wall Street Journal*, provides business news, as we might expect. Also available, however, is general news, New York news, U.S. government news, news from foreign countries, and specialized news covering a few dozen industries, from "Accounting" to "Utilities." The charges are $12 per hour ($60 per hour during prime time).

Information provided includes:

1. Current market quotations on stocks, bonds, options, and warrants (with a 15-minute delay)

2. General news, "as recent as 90 seconds and as old as 90 days"

3. Exhaustive information on over 3,000 compa-

nies, all of those listed on the New York Stock Exchange, American Exchange, and 800 over-the-counter stocks, including:

A. Current stock price, prices during the last trading week, and prices during the past 4, 13, and 52 weeks

B. Price changes compared to Standard & Poor's 500 Stock Index

C. Price-earnings ratios for the current year, five-year high, low, and average

D. Earnings for the year, earnings per share for the past 12 months, percentage change from previous quarter, five-year growth rates

E. Price volatility as measured by two favorite barometers of the Wall Streeters, called the "Gain Index" and the "Beta Factor"

F. Much, much more.

I have a feeling that this service will eventually replace the individual files maintained by private investors in thousands of homes across the country.

NewsNet™

This service provides access to over a hundred newsletters, nearly all of which also appear in print. Most of the newsletters are business-oriented, although some cover entertainment subjects. NewsNet, located in Bryn Mawr, PA, is owned by Independent Publications, which also owns local newspapers and once owned the now defunct *Philadelphia Bulletin*.

There's no registration fee. Searching or scanning a newsletter costs $24 per hour. The charges for reading a newsletter vary; they're lower if you are a subscriber to the printed edition.

Users can get information before it's available in

printed form. There's also an "archival service," which allows users to retrieve newsletter information all the way back to January 1982.

NewsNet offers an "electronic clipping service." You supply a keyword and NewsNet searches for it as new information comes into the data base. You may also search the historical data base for keywords.

Newsletter categories include advertising and marketing, aerospace, chemical, energy, entertainment and leisure, health and hospitals, international, and taxation. Some of the non-business-oriented newsletters are *The Gold Sheet* (football betting statistics and recommendations), *The Fearless Taster* (wine-tasting), *Behavior Today*, *Marriage and Divorce*, and *Sexuality Today*.

Other Info Companies

Dialog Information Retrieval Service™ (from Lockheed) makes about 150 data bases available to subscribers. You can get summaries of articles in newspapers, magazines, scientific journals, and trade publications, as well as all kinds of statistical information. The hourly charge ranges from $30 to over $100.

Users may enter keywords and search through data bases for information on particular subjects. Most information is summarized; you may order a complete copy of the text through the service, which is sent by U.S. mail.

There are about 1,500 data bases in the United States. Most of them cover specific subjects not of interest to the average home computerist. Just about any subject you can think of is covered. To give you a small sampling:

1. Mergers and Acquisitions—information on all

publicly announced corporate combinations since the beginning of 1981

2. AMA/NET (American Medical Association)—medical articles and data on 1,500 drugs

3. Advertising and Marketing Intelligence—market research data and information on advertising campaigns

4. Westlaw—legal precedents

5. AgriVisor—farm prices and weather conditions

6. Billboard Information Network—*Billboard Magazine* record charts, available in advance of the printed edition

I recently became convinced that the Era of Information Services is here. In a computer magazine, a columnist asked his readers to correspond with him. Did he list a mailing address? No. A telephone number? Not a chance. He gave his Source and CompuServe "addresses"!

Chapter 6

Video Entertainment:
Home Computer Games

Many hundreds of video games have been produced for home computers. Indeed, I suspect game-playing is often the primary reason for buying a home computer. No doubt many home computers, purchased initially to perform other functions, are used solely for game-playing.

The viable game-playing computers include the Atari®, Apple®, VIC 20™, TI-99/4A™, and TRS-80® Color Computer (Coco). Most Timex 1000™ games are trivial because of the limitations of this tiny computer. The other computers covered in this book have either few really good games or virtually no games at all. In this chapter, I'll discuss how well the five major game-playing computers perform this function.

If your interest is solely in game-playing, you should consider the purchase of one of the home video systems. The most popular system to date has been the Atari VCS™; over ten million have been sold. Several hundred game cartridges have been produced for this system by Atari and approximately 30 other game producers. The days of the Atari VCS may be numbered, however, since all the VCS games may now also be played on Coleco's ColecoVision™ and Mattel®'s Intellivision II™, both of which are superior to the VCS.

Atari®

The Atari computers are the kings of the game computers. Many Atari computer games are the very best that can be played at home, bar none.

If the Video Academy Awards were held, Atari would win the prize for "Best Home Adaptation of Popular Coin-operated Games," with its authentic renditions of *PAC-MAN*® (far better than the unacceptable Atari VCS version), *Missile Command*®, *Space Invaders*®, and *Centipede*®.

Many exciting, addictive non-arcade games are also available for the Atari computers. Heading the list is *Miner 2049er*®, which is so good that some in the industry predict that it'll be the first game to "go the other way"—that is, to start as a home game and be converted into an arcade game.

Countless excellent games are becoming available for the Atari computers, because so many software houses have decided to produce Atari computer games, including some companies that heretofore had made only video-system cartridges, such as Activision® and Imagic®.

One caution: It's important that you check the requirements of each game to ensure it fits on your Atari. Some, for example, require 48K and a disk drive. You need not be concerned about which Atari computer you own. All Atari games can be played on the 400®, 800®, or 1200XL®.

Apple®

The sounds one hears when playing many Apple II® computer games remind me of an indelicate function of the human body. But the colors are superior, and many games are fabulous. There are an enormous number—hundreds—of games for the Apple computer. They vary from very poor to phenomenal.

Many Apple games can get addictive. I daresay a lot of people who own Apples spend more time playing games than they'd be willing to admit. The better games are intricate and detailed—far more so than is technologically possible on home video systems. Two software houses provide about the best Apple games that can be found, Sirius® (Sacramento, CA) and Brøderbund® (San Rafael, CA).

VIC 20™

Many thousands of VIC 20s were sold in 1982 and the first half of 1983. Indeed, Commodore celebrated the production of the millionth VIC 20 at the January 1983 Consumer Electronics Show. This, of course, did not go unnoticed, and software houses are stumbling over themselves to produce VIC 20 games.

The games produced by Commodore itself for the VIC 20 are mediocre. But the big news is that there is an "interface module" (what a horrible name) that allows Atari VCS cartridges to be played on the VIC 20. This means that the VIC has a unique ability among home computers—the 200-plus Atari VCS games can be played on the VIC 20. In my opinion, this feature alone greatly enhances the value of the VIC.

I talked to the president of the company that is manufacturing this adapter. The company was so secretive about this product (no doubt because of Atari's patent-infringement lawsuit against Coleco, which has a similar adapter that allows VCS games to be played on the ColecoVision) that they displayed it, by invitation only, in the bedroom of a Las Vegas motel. If you're interested, here's the information:

Cardapter/1—suggested list price $90
Cardco, Inc.
3135 Bayberry
Wichita, KS 67226

Another company also advertises this product in the computer and video magazines—Protecto Enterprizes (sic) of Barrington, IL. It is a distributor for Cardco.

When we consider the vast number of games being produced for the Atari VCS and the many, many games that will be produced by Commodore and third-party vendors for the VIC, it is possible that VIC may eventually challenge the Atari computers as the top game-playing home computer. That is to say, while the VIC 20 won't match the graphics and sound of the Atari computers, it may surpass them because of sheer game volume alone.

TI-99/4A™

The TI-99/4A games enable the person who bought the 99/4A for other purposes to have some fun playing games. I would advise against buying a 99/4A solely for game-playing, however. Other computers far surpass this one in the games category.

The word for 99/4A games is "acceptable." The graphics (color, sound, and detail of characters) are acceptable; the sound effects are acceptable; the joystick controls are OK; most of the games are of average interest. Some games can be played on a TI sound synthesizer (which lists for about $150), which gives you a talking computer. All cartridges can be played without the synthesizer.

TRS-80® Color Computer

In general, the games made for the Coco are below average. The more acceptable ones are designed by third-party houses, not by Radio Shack.

The Coco falls short as a game-playing computer. The controls are terrible, the screen displays only average graphics, and in the several dozen games I reviewed for this book I even found occasional glitches in the game programs.

The joystick is not self-centering, which means that when you get your man or ship or cannon moving, you must return the joystick to the center position before the object stops moving—and even then, it may not. The metallic Coco joystick has an uncontrollable loose feeling that prevents the player from having tight control over the object he's maneuvering on the screen.

The Coco is far surpassed in game-playing ability by other home computers and even by the major home video systems. If your primary interest is in games, forget the Coco.

Chapter 7

Other Entertainment:
Bridge, Chess, Checkers,
and Other Non-Video Games

Computers are instructive in areas not ordinarily thought of as learning, namely in helping us to gain skills in the nonelectronic games that have constituted entertainment in American homes for decades. I'm referring to such games as chess, bridge, backgammon, and othello.

Computer learning in these areas developed earlier than in the more conventional forms of education. I suspect this is because games such as bridge and chess have proved their popularity; it's known that they have a wide following. Thus they offer more immediate commercial potential.

Learning these types of games is part of the educational process for many. There is no doubt that bridge is considered in many circles a "social skill." Such games as chess and backgammon can require the use of intense inductive logic, an ability that contributes to success in "more serious" areas of human endeavor.

In other words, it's not totally clear where "real learning" begins and game-playing ends. I don't profess to know the answer. The point remains, however, that computers can help us learn these "games" quite well.

Have home computers been successful in helping teach entertainment skills? So far, I'd rank industry efforts with a B in this category. Much has been done so far; more could be done.

The most impressive programs of this type cover the cerebral pursuits, such as chess, bridge, othello, cribbage, and gin rummy. Thanks to computers, you can now play these games whenever you want a game "fix." There's no need to look for a partner or a fourth for bridge. More important, the computer teaches— by suggesting moves and evaluating your play.

In some areas, I question the usefulness of the software. For example, I cannot understand why anyone would spend $40 or so for a program to be able to play the card game solitaire with a computer. I should think using real cards would be more fun—and in fact faster (you could conceivably improve at the game if the computer pointed out errors in your play, but the solitaire software I've seen does not have this feature).

Nor can I understand why anyone would want to spend time in such pursuits as computer craps, roulette, and bingo. Absolutely no skill is required. Contrary to the wishful thinking of "systems" players (mostly broke, I would guess), it is fruitless to practice these games to increase one's chances of winning in a casino—or at the local church.

There's software to play checkers (good), blackjack (good), and dominoes (average), to solve Rubik's Cube (OK), and even to make up crossword puzzles (average). There are programs to play hearts, baccarat (senseless, in my opinion), various forms of poker (even a strip-poker package, which is basically a one-joke program), and, would you believe, go fish.

Home computers are not uniquely able to help you play these games. In some areas, they face strong competition from the lowly video game systems. To wit:

Bridge—excellent game developed for the Atari®
VCS™ by Activision®

Backgammon—instructive simulation for Mattel®'s Intellivision™

Blackjack—good cartridge by Atari; poor ones from
Mattel and Odyssey®

Checkers—Intellivision has a superior checkers,
Atari an average one

Othello—excellent games by both Atari and Emerson® (for the VCS and Arcadia-2001™ systems)

Chess—an average game for the Atari VCS (in
chess, the video systems cannot compete with
home computers)

Unfortunately, most of the better computer programs cannot be run on a $300 computer system.
Many require disk drives and, in some cases, more
memory than comes with the computer. Some of the
best software in this category is for the Atari computers (close to $1,000 or more with disk drive) and
the Apple IIe™ (which starts at over $1,000 without
disk drive).

Chess

There's no doubt that one can find a good game
of chess with a computer—and that the computer will
help you to learn the game, and learn it fast. Most
computer chess programs have one basic problem:
They play rapidly at lower skill levels, but at higher
levels, they may take hours to make a move. Unless
you're a real chess master, however, the chances are
you'll be able to find a challenging game that won't
take weeks to complete.

Let's say that you like to play chess. How happy
would you be if you had an opponent that permitted
the following?

1. You could play against him at any time, day or night, rain or shine. He'd never be too tired or not feel like playing.

2. At your command, he would play like a beginner, like an expert, or at any one of a dozen intermediate skill levels.

3. If you asked him, he'd suggest moves to you (and not bad moves in order to beat you).

4. He'd play against himself at various skill levels. Thus, at higher levels, you could effectively watch as two experts competed.

5. You could play him blindfolded and he wouldn't get angry if you beat him (I never really believed anyone could do that until my roommate beat me, never looking at the board; it's humiliating, to say the least).

6. He'd tell you what moves he was considering, and in total candor tell you what moves he suspected you were contemplating!

Sound like a chess buff's dream? Well, there's a program available that provides this. Your opponent, of course, is a computer. It's *CHESS*, by Odesta®, Evanston, IL. It costs $70 and can be run on the Apple II™ or Atari computers. The Odesta version takes full advantage of the computer's capabilities and provides the chess addict with about all he could want to experiment, to play, and, above all, to learn!

Chess programs are available for the less expensive computers. One, designed for the TI-99/4A™, costs $70 and does not have all the features of the Odesta program. But it's satisfactory, offers different skill levels and several computer playing strategies (i.e., aggressive or defensive), can play up to nine different opponents, and can be used to solve chess problems.

Sargon II Chess™ ($40 from Commodore) is an excellent chess program for the VIC 20™. It has seven difficulty levels and allows you to sit back, use a joy-stick, and play armchair chess; this is much easier than entering the moves with alphanumeric codes on the computer keyboard. This program has been rated highly by several chess experts.

Bridge

This is an area where home computers have found a need and successfully filled it. Computers can play an excellent game of bridge. Bridge experts will scoff at some of the plays, but most of us beginners and intermediates will be challenged and be provided an opportunity to improve our games.

Computer bridge is particularly helpful to those who want to improve, but don't want to study a dry bridge text or endlessly deal out practice hands. Another advantage is that you can play any time you want; no need to find other players.

Dynacomp, Inc., Rochester, NY, has a program called *Bridgemaster*™ for both the Atari and Apple computers. As in the bridge columns, you are South. The computer becomes your partner (North) and your two opponents (East and West).

You play just as you would in a four-person bridge game. All "players" bid. If you win the bid, you play; the computer defends. If you lose the bid, the computer tries to make the bid and also plays your partner's hand.

The program has shortcomings (limited playing ability and a finite number of hands—1,000), but for $22, many will consider it worthwhile.

Othello

Othello is a popular board game. There's a U.S. Othello Association and national and international competitions. Othello has been described as a game that takes minutes to learn, but a lifetime to master.

Home computers can play othello better than most of us (as can the home video systems, including the Atari VCS and the newer Emerson Arcadia-2001).

Programs allow you to play against the computer at several skill levels. If you are stuck (or even if you're not), you can ask for help, and the computer will suggest moves. You may recall moves, if you change your mind, and save games to be completed later, if desired. Some programs allow you to set up problems and try to solve them (like the chess problems in the newspaper columns).

A couple of good othello programs are *Renaissance*™, by UMI, Pomona, CA, for the VIC 20, and *ODIN*™, by Odesta, Evanston, IL, for Atari and Apple.

Blackjack

Just about every home computer and video system has a version of blackjack.

First, let me emphatically say that I don't believe it's currently possible to make a lot of money playing casino blackjack. I did make a good living at it for about six years. But those days are gone forever. The pit bosses have gotten too smart and are taking countermeasures against the skillful player (such as using eight decks in Atlantic City and shuffling continually in Nevada).

Computer blackjack is for those who want to have fun playing at home, or for those who want to practice to *lose less*. I urge you not to plan on making a career out of "21"; it could be very short, very frustrating, and very expensive!

There are two programs that teach you how to

"count cards," that is, to try to get the edge over the house. One is *Ken Uston's Professional Blackjack*™ (Intelligent Statements, Chapel Hill, NC). I licensed a doctor who became totally fascinated with computers (and with blackjack), David Handel, to incorporate my card-counting techniques into a blackjack program. I'll try to be objective and simply say that David and his programmers did an excellent job of translating the card-counting systems from my book *Million Dollar Blackjack* to their software. The program allows the player to practice card-counting, while playing hands. It gives the player the correct "count" and steps him through the proper way to play the hands. The program is available for the IBM Personal Computer™. David tells me that he's planning to produce an Apple II version as well.

The World's Greatest Blackjack Program™, (Apple Special Delivery®) is the other card-counting program. The title is somewhat overblown, but this program does teach the user how to card-count, with appropriate training drills.

Several programs don't teach card-counting, but provide a means of learning basic blackjack by playing against the computer. The best of these is *Apple 21*™ (Softape®, North Hollywood, CA). *Apple 21* is an authentic adaptation of blackjack. The player has all the options offered in most casinos, including splitting and resplitting pairs (identical cards) and taking the insurance bet if the dealer has an ace upcard. This excellent program, as you might guess, was designed for use on Apple II computers.

There are several poor versions of computer blackjack. Among these are *Blackjack*, by Atari for the Atari computers, and *The Gambler*™, by Timex® for the Timex 1000™. Both programs are unacceptable approximations of the actual game.

Checkers

Yes, you can play this classic game against the computer—and learn quite a bit in the process. As in chess, the computer moves slowly at the higher skill levels, but the wait isn't nearly as long as in chess.

You can play anytime you want against an opponent of varying skills. In some programs, the computer will give you advice, and you can watch it play against itself, learning in the process.

Checkers ($50) (Odesta, Evanston, IL) incorporates all of the above features in a program designed for the Atari and Apple. *Checker King*™ (Atari Program Exhange, Sunnyvale, CA) is cheaper ($23), but has fewer features. You get what you pay for.

Cribbage

Here again, you can learn a game quickly by observing the computer play against you and, of course, by playing yourself and seeing what works and what doesn't.

An effective version of cribbage is included in the package *The Card Stars*™ (Datamost Inc., Chatsworth, CA). The game plays much faster than regular cribbage because of the speed of the computer in shuffling the "cards," playing, computing points, and moving the pegs around the simulated cribbage board displayed on the screen.

It's instructive to watch the cards that the computer saves for the crib and how it plays its cards on the field. Options allow you to ask the computer for all combinations of four cards, out of the six you are dealt, to help in deciding which cards to discard for the crib.

An Atari version of cribbage, by Thorn EMI Video

Programmes, New York, NY, requires the player to make the scoring calculations, which is more realistic, but plays slower.

There are many cribbage packages out; some of the better ones include: *Cribbage*, Rainbow Computing, Northridge, CA; *Cribbage II*™, Computek, Canyon Country, CA; *King Cribbage*™, Hayden Book Company, Rochelle Park, NJ; and *Hi-Res Cribbage*™, On Line Systems, Coarsegold, CA.

Gin Rummy

Here again, you can use the computer to improve at gin rummy (and surprise the guys down at the lodge). You can play rapidly and are able to rearrange your hand in any way you choose, and the computer scores the game automatically.

Better programs allow you to conduct "postmortems" by examining the contents of the discard pile and the unused deck. This allows you to evaluate how well you played the hand.

Gin Rummy (Datamost, Chatsworth, CA), has all of the above features. This excellent package has three game options: knock with 10 points or less, knock any time, or play until "gin" is reached (no knocking).

Other Games

By now, I'm sure you understand how computers can teach you to play games like these. You learn by playing, but also by observing how the computer plays. In many cases, the computer instructs you by identifying preferred moves or plays.

There are too many programs to list here. Software that may be of interest includes:

Backgammon: Several programs help you learn, including *Fast Gammon*™, by Quality Software, Reseda, CA (for Atari and Apple computers); *Backgammon 2.0*™ for Atari (available on cassette or diskette) by Dynacomp, Rochester, NY; and *Color Backgammon*™ by Radio Shack for the Coco.

Poker: Programs include *Poker Tourney*™ (draw poker) by Artworx, Fairport, NY, for Atari computers; and *Poker Party*™ (draw poker), by Dynacomp, Rochester, NY, for Apple, Atari, and Radio Shack Coco computers.

Software can be purchased with which you may play hearts, go fish, and variations of the popular board game Master Mind. Programs can construct crossword puzzles from words you furnish (*Crossword Magic*™, by L + S Computerware, Sunnyvale, CA), let you play dominoes, or teach you to solve Rubik's Cube (this one is essentially free; the program listing is published in *Microcomputing* magazine, December 1982).

You can also play Monopoly®, Scrabble®, or Mah-Jongg. If you choose (and I'm not encouraging it), you can buy software to play solitaire, craps, roulette, and baccarat.

Home computers can help you become more adroit at numerous games. The programs that capitalize best on the computer's capability are those that analyze hundreds or thousands of alternative decisions for you, as in the games of chess and bridge.

There's little doubt that future computer programs in this category will be vastly improved as programming techniques become more refined and greater computer capacity becomes readily available. Future programs will play more competently against you (increasing your inferiority complexes even more). They'll require less waiting time and contain even more effective teaching aids.

Chapter 8

Other Home Uses:
Music, Art, Filing, Health, and Other

Music

The music programs currently available for the smaller computers are poor. There is no viable music software for the Timex 1000™. Commodore produces a cartridge which allows you to use the VIC 20™ as a music keyboard and "play" notes, but the program is rudimentary.

TI Music Maker™, for the 99/4A, is an average music program that allows the user to select notes, using a cursor, and place them on a musical staff that is printed on the screen. The user may choose whole, half, quarter, eighth, and sixteenth notes, and can create harmony by entering up to three musical lines.

A second feature of this program allows the user to select frequencies, from 110 to 20,000 hertz cycles per second. This option is more a curiosity than a practical musical exercise (the sounds at around 20,000 cycles will drive your dog wild).

Better musical programs for the low-cost computers are coming. One successful musical attempt is being developed by Mattel® for its Intellivision II/ Computer Adaptor™ equipment. For about $70, a full-size four-octave keyboard attachment and a *Melody Maker*™ cartridge will be available. The user plays the keyboard like a piano, and the musical notation miraculously appears in living color on the screen. Transposition is possible, so that a budding Chopin can enter a song in the easy key of C major, push a button or two, and see his melody written in G-flat, B-natural, or any other key.

Several average music programs have been produced for the Atari® computers, including *Advanced Musicsystem*™, by the Atari Program Exchange, and *Music Compose*™, by Atari. The user enters music using the computer keyboard, and it is converted to musical notation on the screen. Both programs let the user play back his creations on Atari's superior sound system.

ALF Music Synthesizer™

This is one of the most impressive music "writing" programs. But you get what you pay for, and, in this case, you need an Apple II™ computer (either the II, II+, or IIe version) with disk drive, an external audio amplifier, and $200 to buy the music "board" (which fits into a slot at the rear of the computer) and the program disk.

A blank treble and bass clef appear on the screen. Using paddle controllers, you guide cursors around the screen to select notes. A selection display is shown at the bottom of the screen, from which you pick the length of note you want and sharps, flats, or naturals, if desired.

You may set the time (3/4, 4/4, or even 7/4, 9/4, or others) and the key signature. You may vary the volume and timbre of each note. Up to nine voices may be entered.

When the song is played back, a colorful display shows an attractive music continuum for each voice, as the notes dance around the screen. You select the playback speed, which, unlike conventional recording equipment, varies without changing the pitch of the song. This program also utilizes the lightning-fast speed of the computer to allow instantaneous transposition. It's quite impressive to write a song in one key, hit a key on the keyboard, and watch as the song is displayed in another key, in seconds.

Does the *AFL Music Synthesizer* have any practical application? There are several possibilities:

1. The piano student who wants to hear how a piece is supposed to sound, as he's struggling to learn it, could program it into the computer and listen to it— at any number of speeds and in any key.

2. Someone learning an instrument (say a trumpet or clarinet) can create accompaniment as he's learning new tunes, by programming in three or four voices and playing along with them.

3. A music hobbyist who can't play piano can create music by entering music and "playing" the computer.

4. A music arranger can experiment with different voicings and have them automatically documented. (While the experimentation portion is far faster if done on a piano, the documentation is another thing.)

5. Music hobbyists interested in experimenting with different or unusual time signatures will find this program a valuable tool. Composers will be able to try various musical configurations to hear how they sound (for example, one might enter in a phrase and repeat it, transposed up a third, fifth, seventh, and ninth, and play back all voices simultaneously).

Those who are interested in music won't have trouble finding uses for the *ALF Music Synthesizer*. More likely, the problem will be finding the time to experiment with *ALF*; this program could easily provide hundreds of hours of captivating creativity.

Art

As anybody who has seen the movie *Tron* is aware, computers can be used to create a wide variety of unusual and dramatic graphics effects. Home computer programs can convert the computer into a coloring book or a doodling pad. You can also create complex multicolored patterns that would be virtually impossible to duplicate manually.

Micro Painter™ for the TI-99/4A is an electronic coloring book, pure and simple. Pictures appear on the screen, and the child (I presume) colors them in. *Delta Drawing*™ (Spinnaker Software, Belmont, MA) allows Apple computer users to create images on the screen and color them in. This program, too, is designed for children.

Micro-Painter (Datasoft®, Charsworth, CA) is an innovative program that allows the user to create line drawings and in color, using up to twenty-one colors. The package includes an option which provides a close-up view of the "dots" on the screen, so that the computer artist can color each dot individually, making the creation of highly intricate, colorful images possible.

If you happen to be into symmetry, *Kaleidoscope* (Artworx™, Fairport, NY) lets you design kaleidoscope patterns with an Atari computer, in living color.

Personal Filing Systems

Using personal filing software, you may enter information into a computer system, store it, and recall portions of it that you want, using key words. These programs will tend to appeal to those who are methodical and enjoy keeping track of things. Filing-system programs usually require large amounts of computer memory and a disk system. Several examples:

Kitchen recipes: The user may type in recipes and summon the ones in a given category, such as "seafood," "chicken," "canapés," or even all meals in which Béarnaise sauce is an ingredient. These programs could prove invaluable to inveterate cooks who own dozens of cookbooks and would prefer to consolidate their confusing array of references into a single file. The initial data entry, however, is likely to be onerous and time-consuming.

Personal library: I have a classmate who collects books—he's got thousands of them. He uses his Apple computer to keep track of his library and to get listings of all books by a given author or publisher, or on any topic (e.g., World War II, the Mafia, contemporary poets, etc.).

Personal collections: Listing programs can be used to keep track of virtually any type of personal collection, such as records, stamps, coins, or, for that matter, software. They can also record names, addresses, and other data for Christmas lists and other mailings. I suspect, however, that for most people a good old card filing system or simply a handwritten list would suffice.

Programs available: The thrifty computerist can find free listings of programs in the "public domain." Two such library programs are *Bookshelf Database* for Apple computers (*Microcomputing*, November 1982) and an IBM Personal Computer library program (*Microcomputing*, December 1982).

There are generalized filing programs which file and recall virtually any type of information. Two such programs are *Filemanager*™ for Atari computers (Synapse Software, Richmond, CA) and *PFS: Personal Filing*™ for Apple II computers (Software Publishing, Mountain View, CA).

Other Areas

Health

Diet analysis: You enter your intake of food and are given information on the number of calories eaten and statistics on fiber, fat, protein, vitamins, and minerals (*Nutricheck*™, WIMS, Tulsa, OK).

Personal Fitness Program™ (Atari Program Exchange) has you type in your age, sex, and pulse rate. The program steps you through eight exercises, for which it computes the proper speed, based on your current physical condition. You need not exercise alone: A little character on the screen runs through the routine with you, governing the speed and the number of repetitions.

Astrology

You tell the computer when and where you were born, and the program calculates your astrological "chart" (*Astroscope*™, AGS Software, for Apple II computers). Another program draws your chart on the screen; you may also print it, if you desire (*Astrology*, Atari Program Exchange for Atari computers).

Biorhythms

You enter your birthdate, and the computer tells you about your physical, emotional, and intellectual cycles for any given day. Experimenting with this package might prove enlightening and amusing. Imagine, for example, entering Napoleon's birthdate and telling the computer that today is the date of Waterloo (*Biorhythms*, for the Timex 1000; *Biorhythm*, for and by Atari).

Crossword puzzles

The user can give the computer words to be included in a crossword puzzle (using, say, a particular theme). The computer generates a bona fide crossword. The user then constructs the clues (*Cross Magic 2.0*℠, for Atari and Apple II computers, by L&S Computerware, Sunnyvale, CA).

Genealogy

You can keep track of your ancestors, gradually adding biographical information as it's unearthed by your research. This must be a popular field, because there are over a dozen genealogy programs, many of which are listed in *Personal Computing*, January 1983.

Other Personal Uses

By now, you're probably getting the idea. Just about any subject that involves data being calculated, stored, or retrieved can be made into a computer program.

The chances are that if you're interested in a given field, you'll find a program about it.

A brief sampling:

Convert weights and measurements or calculate the ingredients needed for various numbers of portions. One simplistic but inexpensive program is *Converting Measurements*, in *The Timex Personal Computer Made Simple* (Signet, 1982).

Take an IQ test (something many of us have been curious, or perhaps petrified, about). IQ programs have been produced for both children and adults. One is *Know Your Own IQ*™, by Commodore for the VIC 20.

Analyze your handwriting. The user types in handwriting characteristics and receives a personality analysis, just as in the carnivals.

For those who are both oversexed and unimaginative, there's even a program which, given your sexual proclivities, suggests "interludes" that you might try. This is not a children's program (*Interlude*™, Syntonic Software, Houston, TX).

Some programs claim to be able to help you win at the races or by betting on football. (I gambled for a living for six years—at blackjack—and do *not* recommend them.)

For those who dream of winning a fortune at the races, System Design Lab (Redondo Beach, CA) has designed a program in which you enter information about the horses in a race and which track they're running at. The computer chews on this information and spews out handicapping information.

Other programs (such as *Pro Football* and *College Football*, System Design Lab) analyze information on football teams and point spreads and provide the user with betting recommendations.

Computers and the House

Yes, it is true that computers can be used to raise your shades in the morning, turn on your coffee machine, and tell you what appointments you have scheduled during the day. They can also regulate the temperature of your house, detect intruders and turn on the lights to intimidate them, and activate your hot tub at 7:30 P.M. to the water temperature of your choice.

These uses are not widely available, especially for the owner of one of the cheaper home computers. It is inevitable that these types of products will become more readily available in the future. The people who enjoy such electronic amenities are largely computer hobbyists who like to experiment in this area.

Parenthetically, and irrelevantly, the founder of Atari, Nolan Bushnell, introduced a computer robot at the January 1983 Consumer Electronics Show. Bob, as the robot is called, will follow people (he responds to heat from human bodies). He also "talks," using preprogrammed phrases or sentences. Nolan promises much more sophisticated robots in the future, ones that will fetch drinks or vacuum the house. He'll make a million if he invents one that does windows.

Chapter 9

How to Buy Software

Quite recently, it was difficult to get an evaluation of the quality of many software packages. Worse yet, purchasers not infrequently would buy programs with glitches (programmers call them "bugs") in them that wouldn't do what they were supposed to do. Fortunately, that's rapidly changing because of the exploding popularity of home computers.

Don't get me wrong. There are some terrible packages around. Some that are currently being produced still have bugs. Others are misrepresented by their advertising, which claims that programs will help you do things that they really can't do. Still other software, though not misrepresented, is of questionable practical value.

Here are the best ways to find good software:

Computer Magazines

More and more computer magazines are emphasizing the review and evaluation of software. General magazines, such as *Creative Computing* and *Popular Computing*, often do this by subject area. So if you want to know what's available in (say) home finance, music, or children's education, you can often find a magazine issue dedicated to one of these subjects. Some computer magazines (including *Creative Computing* and *PC*) publish special software buyer's guides periodically.

Other magazines are published for the users of

specific computers, such as the Coco, Apple®, IBM PC, and Timex 1000™. These magazines not only evaluate software, but often print program listings that allow you to build your software library for the cost of the magazine, if you have the patience and time to type in the program instructions.

The appendix of this book describes the better computer magazines and tells how to get them. Back issues serve as excellent reference. Several magazines print annual listings of all articles appearing each year, by subject area. Many readers of computer magazines save their back issues, for good reason.

Books

More and more books are being published that evaluate specific computer programs. Several of the best are:

The Book of Apple Software, 1983, The Book Company, Los Angeles, CA. The publishers state that every Apple II™ owner who buys software should have a copy of this book. I thoroughly agree. It gives complete ratings of hundreds and hundreds of Apple programs, usually in clear language. Program reviews are organized by major user category (such as education, games, etc.). The book is reissued annually.

The Book of Atari Software, 1983 (same publisher) is just as excellent. It's not as thick as the Apple guide because there's currently more Apple software. But just wait awhile. A flood of Atari® programs is now being produced.

Commodore Software Encyclopedia, Commodore Business Machines, Inc., King of Prussia, PA. This book lists hundreds of programs for the VIC 20™ and other Commodore computers used primarily in schools and businesses. It is not nearly as helpful as the two books mentioned previously because the program descriptions are brief and no evaluations are included. However, the programs are arranged by subject, and prices and names and addresses of vendors are included.

Software/Hardware Directory and Guide (Micro Software, Quincy, IL) and *The Directory of Independent IBM Personal Computer Hardware and Software* both evaluate IBM PC software. The former is updated every six months.

Applications Software Sourcebook is an inexpensive book which discusses hundreds of programs written for Radio Shack® computers.

It's just a matter of time before books evaluating software for the Timex 1000, TI-99/4A®, and other home computers become available.

Word-of-Mouth

The chances are good that if you're interested in a specific program, it will have been reviewed in a magazine or book. Most of the good ones are. However, if you can't find anything, ask around and get word-of-mouth advice about the category of software you're interested in. It's likely that others share your interest. Contact local computer clubs. Hang around your local computer center and talk to other customers. Call on computer stores. If you're tied into one of the information services (or know someone who is), use that source. Groups of people who share common interests often have "meetings" using CompuServe® or Source℠.

Software-of-the-Month Clubs

These clubs offer discounts to those who buy a minimum number of software packages. While they do not appear to preview individual programs before they're included in their offering, they usually pick "brand-name" products from established vendors.

Evaluating Software Manufacturers

Look at software houses the way you do book authors. If a vendor has come out with one good program, chances are that most of that company's line is also good. There are, of course, exceptions to this rule. The larger houses that advertise regularly in the major computer magazines generally supply reliable product; their success didn't come from producing shoddy programs with bugs.

It's best to try a program *before* you buy it. This is obviously impossible if you're buying by mail order. (Do *not* buy an unknown piece of software by mail order.) But if the package is sold by a local computer store, the manager will usually let you run it for a while to test it out. You may be able to borrow a program from a computer club or computer-owning friend.

As you can see, there are many ways to check out software before you buy. And the good news is that because of the growing demand for software evaluations, more and more are continually becoming available.

Backup Software and Piracy

Software is a lot easier to ruin than a phonograph record. Cassette tapes break and stretch. A little oil or grease on the exposed part of a floppy disk can render it worthless. To protect against these disasters, users often make "backup copies" of their tapes or disks, which is quite easy to do.

This practice has led to abuse. Software "pirates" make copies and sell or give them away to others. This cuts into the profits of manufacturers and forces them to take countermeasures. Many now "copy protect" their software, which prevents users from making backup copies.

This isn't a bad solution, but what happens when a user legitimately needs a backup copy in the event he "clobbers" the original? Some vendors allow original purchasers to obtain additional copies free or at a low price. But what happens if the software is ruined in the middle of an important project and the user can't wait weeks to get a replacement copy?

Software manufacturers, retailers, and pirates all get pretty emotional about this issue. Manufacturers complain that the vast majority of software users obtained their programs illicitly. Retailers insist that many users, even schools, routinely break the law in this area (it *is* a violation of copyright laws to make copies of software for others). One retailer noted sadly that when one school district bought a piece of educational software, copies suddenly appeared in every school in the district.

The pirates attempt to justify their behavior by claiming that software is absurdly expensive. There's even a counterculture of pirates who delight in thwarting the latest copy-protection scheme. Some are so proud of their handiwork in "cracking the code" that they personalize their copies with by-lines such as "Cracked by Mr. Xerox" or "Fixed by the Mechanic."

Just imagine if people could make copies of phonograph records on some kind of copying device for a dollar. That's the kind of problem present here. It's difficult to predict how this controversy will be resolved. Perhaps the price of software will gradually come down until it's almost as expensive to copy it and reproduce the accompanying user's manual.

What *is* important is that you should be sure to have access to backup copies so that your programs can be run when you want to run them.

SECTION II

WHICH COMPUTER IS FOR YOU?

In this section, I address the question that so many have been asking lately: "What computer should I buy?"

Because of the explosion in the home computer market, there have been numerous articles in newspapers and magazines giving advice on this question. Most of them give good general advice, but don't get specific enough. For example, this is their basic advice:

1. Know what you want the computer to do.

2. Look at the software first, not the hardware, to ensure that you don't end up with a machine that cannot run the programs you want.

3. Consider how much you can afford to spend, but don't make your decision based solely on price. A "bargain" computer may end up gathering dust in a garage or closet.

I couldn't agree more with this advice. But it's also possible to explain which computer is best for various types of jobs and to make specific recommendations to you. I will do that in this section.

Remember, however, that selecting a computer *is* personal. I'm not trying to hedge on these recommendations, but the plain fact is that some people enjoy Johnny Carson and others prefer Dick Cavett; some would rather have air conditioning in their car instead of cruise control; some golfers like the feel of Wilson irons and others like Spaldings.

After you've considered the pluses and minuses

listed for each computer, go out and try the one you think may be for you. Find out how you like the feel of the keyboard, the display on the screen, or, if it's important to you, the color of the console.

For our purposes, we'll define a home computer as one that is used primarily for game-playing or for home applications, and that can be bought (in stripped-down but usable form) for $200 or less. In order of price (don't hold me to this—you never know when some wild discounter will come up with an Atari® mega-sale), they are:

HOME COMPUTER	PRICE	MARKET SHARE
Timex Sinclair 1000™	$ 40–100	26%
VIC 20™	80–300	23
TI-99/4A™	100–200	23
Atari® 400	80–300	17
TRS-80® Color Computer	200–300	10

There are other home computers to be sure, such as the Timex 2000®, TI-99/2, and Panasonic JR-200U. For various reasons, these are less likely to be of interest to the first-time computer user, but they are described briefly at the end of this section.

So that you know what choices others are making, I have shown, in the table above, the estimated percentage that each has of the total home computer market (per the Yankee Group, an industry analyst). These figures, however, are continually changing.

The prices listed are for the basic computer. It's possible to spend hundreds of dollars more on accessories, the most common of which are disk drives, printers, monitors, and modems. All of the computers listed can be attached to your television set.

I have included seven more computers in this survey. None of them fits into the above definition of home computers, but they may be of interest to you for various reasons:

COMPUTER	PRICE
Commodore 64™	$250–595
Atari® 800™	380–750
Atari 1200XL™	460–900
Apple IIe™	1,300–1,400
IBM Personal Computer™ (PC)	1,300

and two interesting portable computers:

Osborne I™	$1,295–1,795
KayPro II	1,595–1,795

In the introduction to Section I, I mentioned that usable RAM is measured in something called K. The following should give you an idea of how much K you need:

> 2K—too small to be of use to almost any of us
> 4—very small, but not quite as bad
> 16—OK; a lot of programs can run on this
> 48—good; just about all games can fit, as can most programs for home use
> 64—luxury, like 400 horsepower in a car
> over 64—a waste of money for you and me

There's one more measure that those of you considering using a computer to write should be aware of. That's the number of columns (characters across) that a computer shows on its display screen. Here are some guidelines:

22 columns—no good for writing, period

32   —OK for about two letters a month

40   —OK for average high school or college writing, or for an occasional article

52 or 64   —you can write books with this, but it's much nicer to have:

80   —good enough for all writers I know

Chapter 10

Timex® Sinclair 1000™

$40–100   2K standard; expandable
to 16K or more

You Should Buy One If:

A. You can't afford to spend more than $50 ($100
if you don't own a cassette recorder), you own a TV,
and you want to:

—run rudimentary programs to keep your budget,
balance your checkbook, keep lists of things on cassette tape or perform similar household functions,

—find out how a computer works, firsthand,
—get into programming
—get your child into programming, and/or
—provide computer math drills for your children

B. You want a low-cost portable computer (battery packs can be purchased for $40 and up).

You Should Not Buy One If:

A. You want to do any of the things in section A above and can afford to spend $80 for a home computer.

B. You want to do word processing, no matter how simple.

C. You want to play video games.

As you can see, there would appear to be a limited market for the Timex 1000. Yet more people currently own one than any other home computer. Company officials are vague about the figure, but it's well over a million units. About one-quarter of all home computers owned are either Timex or its predecessors, the Sinclair ZX80 or ZX81.

Why is this? Because when Timex (or Sinclair) cost $100 to $150, other computers started at $300 or more. The Timex computer will always have its place in the development of home computers as the first bona fide computer available to the public for under $100. The originator of this idea (and of the Timex Sinclair) has become a legend in the industry. He's a Britisher named Clive Sinclair, who was also responsible for developing the first low-cost pocket calculator.

Advertised as the only home computer for under

$100 (which is no longer true), the Timex lists for $99.95. I've seen them on sale for as low as $40 (after manufacturer's rebate).

For this price, almost everything you need is included as long as you have a television set. You must have a cassette recorder as well. An inexpensive battery-powered recorder runs best with the Timex; a powerful system may do it damage. I'd recommend that you use a recorder with a counter (which resembles a car's odometer) in order to keep track of the location of programs on the tape.

The Timex comes neatly packaged in a form-fitting Styrofoam box. You are provided the three required wire connections: one to your TV, one to the cassette recorder, and one to the electrical outlet. In addition, you're supplied with a "transfer switch box," a little black box to be attached to the TV set. Included as well is a comprehensive user's manual that not only tells you how to get the computer running, but also contains a course in elementary programming.

It *is* possible with the Timex 1000 to obtain computer hardware and software to be able to run programs, all for under $100. For those on a tight budget, program listings are available in the user manual. The problem is that the presentation is technical and assumes the user is interested in programming. Thus the average home computer user (and, I presume, most readers of this book) will not find this helpful.

Free programs are listed in the magazine *Sync*, a publication devoted to Timex users. *Sync* is probably available at your local library. A subscription to six bimonthly issues costs $16 (39 E. Hanover Ave., Morris Plains, NJ 07950).

A $3.50 paperback contains program listings to perform various functions, including solving crossword puzzles, conducting spelling bees, balancing a checkbook, and keeping a budget (*The Timex Personal Computer Made Simple*, Signet, 1982).

It's a time-consuming, tedious task to enter program listings into the computer. However, if cost is your dominant concern, you'll find this an economical way to use the computer.

You wouldn't think anything could be bought for a dollar or two in the computer field except batteries, but Timex programs are on sale for these prices. Ezra Group (San Diego, CA), for one, advertises programs with such titles as *Biorhythms*, *Linear Regression*™, and *Random Music! Slow*™ for the price of a pack of cigarettes. I haven't tested them and cannot vouch for them.

If you're considering a Timex, read this paragraph carefully. It is *very* easy to be enticed into spending $200 or more in total. This makes no sense unless you can afford only $40 now and want to expand your computer's capability gradually. For very little more, you can buy a VIC 20™, which, as we will see, is a much better computer (a full-size keyboard with actual keys, color, music, a sturdy casing, and much better software).

To give you an idea of how easy it is to spend more than you plan, let me relate what happened to me when I went in to buy a Timex 1000.

I decided to emulate (a good computer word) the average buyer of a Timex—that is, to question everything as if I knew absolutely nothing (it wasn't difficult). I entered a computer store in New Jersey. In the display case under the cash register was a Timex.

I asked the salesman, "Is it really a computer?"

He said, "Yes, and not only that, you came on a good day. It's on sale for $93."

Neatly laid out near the computer were over a dozen

cassettes for the Timex, with the titles like *The Organizer*®, *Checkbook Analyser*®, and *Loan/Mortgage*®. There were some game cassettes as well.

I asked, "Are those all for the Timex?"

The salesman responded, "Oh, yes. Timex has lots of games and other software."

I popped for the computer, expecting to pay $100 and another $50 or so for a few cassettes, which ranged in price from $14 to $20.

I asked, "How do these cassettes hook into the computer?"

"Well, you need a tape cassette recorder. It's best if it runs on batteries."

"Oh. Do you sell those here?"

"No. We don't."

I ordered five cassettes. The salesman said, "You'll need 16K to run these."

He went on to explain that the basic Timex has only 2K, but that for another $50, I could get a 16K attachment that would allow me to run these programs.

I asked, "Are there any programs that run on the Timex the way it is?"

"Not really. The only thing we have is a *2K Games Pack*®. But it's just games."

I bought the *2K Games Pack* for $15.

I later went to an electronics store, asked for its cheapest battery-operated tape cassette recorder, and found it priced at $31. This salesman said, "But for $39, we have one that can also be plugged in." I bought the $39 model. I also bought a supply of batteries.

So far I'd spent about $175 to be able to run something on "the first computer under $100."

I went home to play the six games in the *2K Games Pack*. Five of the six games in the cassette were trivial—and that's being kind. I couldn't raise the sixth.

"Well," I thought to myself, "be fair. Don't draw any conclusions until you check out the 16K games."

So I went back to the computer store. I bought the 16K attachment for $50 and another $100 worth of cassettes. Now I'd spent $320. Later I found that the best of the 16K games could be rated only as "unacceptable" at best.*

Some of the "serious" Timex cassettes, however, might prove useful to you. For example, the *Vu-Calc*™ program, one of the simplest spreadsheet programs, used correctly, is a fairly effective way to make complex calculations and prepare a series of financial projections under various sets of assumptions.

The Timex has a "membrane-type" keyboard, a flat sheet of plastic, rather than raised keys. The "keys" are small and difficult to operate. The display is limited to black-and-white, and there is no sound.

Many attachments are made for the Timex because so many people own them. There are units to expand it to as much as 64K, keyboards with buttons, battery packs, printers, sound attachments, and hundreds of program cassettes.

The Timex is a bare-bones entry into the world of computing for those on a tight budget. If you restrict your investment to the advertised $100, your computing options are limited. But you do have a bona fide computer.

---

*I've received complaints that the 16K attachment does not fit securely into the console. When the keys are struck, the attachment "jiggles," and the program (and data) can be lost.

Chapter 11

Commodore VIC 20™

| $80–300 | 5K standard (about 3.6K usable); expandable to 70K |

There's no doubt that the VIC, which stands for Video Interface Computer (we'll stick with VIC), has found its place in the market. In fact, looking at the home computer industry, it's fair to say that Christmas 1982 "belonged" to the VIC 20. To give you an idea, 10,000 VICs were sold in all of 1981. How many VICs would you guess were being produced each day at the end of 1982? You guessed it—10,000!

The VIC 20 is the lowest-priced color computer around. It originally listed for $299; now people are paying as little as $80. The VIC is so inexpensive for several reasons: Commodore produces a key component (called a semiconductor microprocessor) itself, which keeps costs down. Also you're getting 5K RAM (only about 3K of which is usable, that is, available for your programs); this is the smallest of any of the home computers except the Timex. The 22-column character display is the narrowest of any of the home computers (including the Timex).

You Should Buy One If:

A. Your primary interest is in games (the one-player variety), but you're considering possibly using your computer for other purposes as well (e.g., budgets, keeping an inventory of things, or maybe even doing a little simple programming).

B. Your child has been using a Commodore PET™ at school, and you want him to have a computer at home to write programs which can be run on his school computer.

You Should Not Buy One If:

A. You want to do word processing.

B. You get the most fun out of those supercompetitive two-player games.

C. Your primary interest is in running home software or in doing some heavy-duty programming.

Key Features of the VIC 20

A. It's a sturdy, good-looking unit with a full-size 64-character keyboard that has a good solid feel when you're typing.

B. There are many games available. This isn't because of the games produced for the VIC 20, which are not that numerous and vary in quality (some are unacceptable). It's because, for $80, you can buy a unit that allows you play the 200-plus Atari® VCS™ games on the VIC (see Chapter 6), and many of these games are fabulous.

C. It has above-average game graphics. The color is acceptable (not up to Atari 400 standards), and the sound effects are effective (there are three voices and a fourth noise generator).

D. It has a socket into which can be plugged any joystick that fits into the Atari VCS. This is good news, because fine joysticks are produced for the VCS (my favorite is the Wico Command Control™). A serious shortcoming of the VIC 20, an inexplicable engineering oversight in my opinion, is that there's only one joystick outlet. Thus only one player can play at a time, and the many fine Atari VCS two-player games cannot be played on the VIC 20.

E. The limited VIC 20 RAM limits the capability of the programs that can be run on the unexpanded VIC 20.

F. Word processing is glum on the VIC. Commodore sells a typing practice and word processing program, but it's not recommended. While the VIC does provide for upper and lower case, its limited memory allows the entering of only about 40 lines of text. The 22-character-per-line screen makes it virtually impossible to do serious writing on the VIC. In fact, the most common complaint of VIC owners is the limited number of characters per line. Quick Brown Fox® has produced a word processing program that is acceptable if an expansion module that allows 40 or 80 columns is also purchased. But without such an attachment, writing on the VIC is best restricted to letters and short literary masterpieces (for the Miltons among you, sonnets, happily, will fit).

G. The VIC has four "programmable" keys. This

is a feature that benefits programmer-users; a programmable key is one that may be assigned a function designated by the user.

Commodore publishes a magazine for owners of its computers, called *Commodore*, of course. It includes articles about Commodore products, helpful hints, and free programs (which must be laboriously typed in).

As is the case for most widely owned computers, you can buy add-ons to do just about anything you want (electronically, that is). Data 20® (Laguna Hills, CA) sells attachments that expand the number of characters per line to 40 or 80 while increasing memory up to as much as 70K (cost: $300 to $400).

To buy an additional 8K costs about $50; 16K is around $100. A Commodore modem, to hook up to outside information sources, runs about $100. There are also joysticks ($20 each), paddle controllers ($20), and disk drives ($400 to $500).

The Commodore people found a gap in the home computer marketplace, and they filled it. There will be a lot of VICs around for a long time to come.

Chapter 12

Texas Instruments 99/4A™

$100–200   16K standard; expandable to 72K

The TI-99/4A is an inexpensive 16K home computer, selling at $200 or less (after manufacturer's rebate). Thanks in large measure to Bill Cosby, it sold well during the latter part of 1982. The quantity of software for the 99/4A was originally limited, because when the computer first came out, TI discouraged others from developing programs for it. The company disregarded the adage that software sells hardware (remember *VisiCalc*®?). The situation has changed. TI has produced some fine software for the 99/4A. A number of other companies are doing so as well.

You Should Buy One If:

A. You want your young child to work with a fine children's computer language, called TI Logo—and you're willing to shell out another $500 on top of the initial investment.

B. You're interested in the 450-program educational package, called Plato Courseware™, that can be run on the TI-99/4A (you'll also need a disk drive, memory expansion, and many Plato software packages).

You Should Not Buy One If:

A. You enjoy home video games and want a wide variety from which to choose.

B. You want to do word processing.

C. You're interested in programming (the TI-99/4A programming language, TI BASIC, is one of the weakest in the industry).

D. You plan eventually to expand your computer system, but want to buy only a "starter" computer now (99/4A add-ons tend to be costly).

The 99/4A presents a representative example of how home computer prices have been dropping. Its predecessor, the 99/4, was introduced at $1,150 (this price included a color monitor). The 99/4A replaced the 99/4, the primary modification being an improved keyboard (a monitor is not required; the unit attaches to home television sets). Not long ago, the 99/4A was selling for over $500.

The 99/4A keyboard has disadvantages. It's narrower than competitive home computers and difficult to operate. The system can accommodate only uppercase, and there are only 32 columns on the screen. For these reasons, this computer is unacceptable for word processing.

The 99/4A is expandable, but at costs which add up fast. For starters, you must spend an additional $40 for an adapter to attach the computer to your television.

The computer has outlets for joysticks (about $35 each). The 99/4A can talk back to you with a vocabulary of several hundred words ($100+). You can get a modem (about $200) or expand to 48K ($300). A disk drive costs about $500, but you must spend another $300 for an attachment that allows it to work.

The 99/4A has good color and three voices plus a noise generator. There are a moderate number of game and home-use cartridges (about fifty), which slide into the front of the console. Far more programs are available for the 99/4A on slow-loading cassette tape and on diskettes.

To take advantage of what I feel is one of its strongest features, the excellent children's TI Logo programming language, you'll have to spend another $500 for the additional memory plus the software.

Texas Instruments publishes a user's newsletter as well as a bimonthly magazine for 99/4A users, called *99'er*. There's also an information service called Texnet℠, available only to 99/4A users.

Chapter 13

TRS-80® Color Computer (Coco)*

$200 to $300   16K standard; expandable
to 32K or more

Once again, let's hear it for competition. The Coco used to sell for $400 and came with 4K or 12K. Now

*Tandy Radio Shack Color Computer is a trademark of the Radio Shack division of Tandy Corporation.

it costs $200 to $300 and 16K is standard. In my view, however, the computer is still overpriced.

The Coco is sold at Radio Shack® stores. You won't see it listed in mail-order catalogs at below list price. There are thousands of Radio Shacks across the country, and they do a good job, by and large, of servicing their computers.

You Should Buy One If:

A. You're quite insecure about getting things serviced and want the comfort of having a manufacturer's store right in your town.

B. There happens to be a Coco software program that you feel you must be able to run (highly doubtful, in my opinion, since Coco programs by and large are mediocre).

You Should Not Buy One If:

A. Your primary (or even secondary) interest is to play video games at home.

B. You want to do word processing.

While the Coco is neatly packaged, it's surprisingly light and doesn't have the durable feel of other comparable computers (most notably the VIC 20™). Its shell is made out of a light plastic material that reminded me of the less sturdy video systems, such as the Odyssey²™.

Radio Shack produces a word processing program for the Coco called *Color Scripsit™ Word Processing*, which sells for $40. While the program itself is complete, there's a serious hardware limitation. The Coco has no lowercase (although there are printers which can be made to print the Coco output in both low-ercase and uppercase) and has only 32 columns across. Furthermore, the keyboard is smaller than that of a regular typewriter and doesn't have the sturdy feel of (say) the VIC 20™ or Atari™ 800. The keys remind me of those on a hand-held calculator. All of these disadvantages preclude serious word processing on the Coco.

The manual that is supplied with the Coco is ex-cellent. It's clearly written, which is quite unusual in this field. It makes effective use of colors and illus-trations. Kids may even read it!

The small children's programming language, Logo, is available for the Coco—at extra cost, of course.

The Coco game situation is glum. Game programs come on cartridges, which are slipped into the side of the console. Game programs are also available on disk-ettes. The games produced by Radio Shack are among the weakest around. Some mediocre games, and a handful of good ones, are produced by third-party houses.

A serious limitation in playing all Coco games lies in the hand controls. The Coco joystick is unwieldy. It's virtually impossible to maintain accurate control over the object you're maneuvering on the screen. On the plus side, there are two joystick outlets, so that two players may compete with each other, as they can't on the VIC 20.

Radio Shack has programs that analyze investments and file and list data. And, of course, there's a calc spreadsheet program; this handles up to 99 columns and 99 rows.

More Americans own the VIC 20, TI-99/4A™, and Atari® computers than they do Cocos. For this reason many third-party software producers are making software for those three computers but not for the Coco. This undoubtedly will widen the gap between these computers and the Coco in the competition for the home computerist's dollar.

Chapter 14

The Atari® Computers

Atari 400™

$80–300   16K standard; expandable
          to 48K or more

Not to be outdone, Atari is doing its share to contribute to the confusion surrounding the home computer industry. Atari has a batch of products on the market—the VCS™, the 5200 Video System, the 400, the 800™, and the 1200XL™.

The Atari 400, the subject of this section, is in my opinion the ultimate game machine under $200.

You Should Buy One If:

A. You want to play the best home computer games available and don't want to spend more than $200.

B. You want to run home software packages only occasionally or do limited programming, in addition to playing games.

You Should Not Buy One If:

A. You want to do word processing.

B. You're much more interested in running home programs (say, for budgeting or keeping electronic files) than you are in playing computer games.

C. You want to do some serious programming.

The 400 is good for game-playing for several reasons. It offers more screen detail than any other computer in its price range; the display has 192 lines of 320 dots each. That provides good animation and close detail.

Color and sound are vital in game-playing. The 400 has 16 colors with 16 intensities of each, giving 256 possible color tones. It has four music voices, allowing songs, in harmony, to accompany the games (this can sometimes become irritating, but the sound volume is adjustable).

The 400 has four outlets for joysticks or paddle controls, located conveniently across the front of the console. The machine also has a slot for game cartridges, at the top of the console.

The most widely played home games are those that are adapted from best-selling arcade games. And Atari leads the PAC with the king of the arcade games (take a guess), as well as *Missile Command*™, *Asteroids*™, *Cen-*

tipede™, and others. Atari also puts out what was the number-one home computer game for many months, *Star Raiders*™.

The Atari 400 was designed to be a fabulous game machine. And it *is* a fabulous game machine.

The 400 hooks up to a standard television; no attachments must be purchased. "Starter kits" are available to get you started in various fields such as home education, communications (to tie into information services), and programming.

Now the bad news. Many of the best games are put out either on cassette tape or diskettes by third-party manufacturers. The cassettes take awhile to load; the diskettes load much more quickly. But to use diskettes requires the purchase of a disk drive, $450 to $500. (The Atari disks are comparatively slow loaders, which is nothing serious generally, but when you need a quick game fix, a few extra seconds of loading time can seem interminable.)

Some diskette games require more than 16K, including some of the better ones (such as *Chop Lifter*™). If your 400 has 48K, you'll be able to play virtually all of the games (at an additional cost of about $200).

Word processing? Forget it. The 40 columns across is not an insurmountable problem. The 400 keyboard is full-size, with 57 keys plus four "special function" keys (they can be programmed to perform various operations desired by the user). The basic problem is that the 400 has a membrane-type keyboard, that is, made of a piece of flat plastic. Even though the membrane has little ridges around each key, and the user hears a beep when each key struck is recorded by the computer, word processing is not a fun thing to do on the 400.

The membrane keyboard doesn't affect game-playing in general, except in playing "adventures," in which the user continually enters phrases to play the game. For most games, you'll play for hours on end without so much as having to touch the keyboard.

In addition to disk drives, other add-ons are available for the 400. You can buy a modem (around $150), a printer, cartridges, joysticks, and paddle controllers. There's even an attachment that converts the 400 into a real keyboard machine (it's sold for $120 by Inhome Software, Mississauga, Ontario, Canada).

If you're serious about programming or want to run home programs extensively, you would be better off considering the Atari 800.

Atari 800™

$380–750   48K standard; expandable
            to 64K or more

The 800 is a 400 with 48K and a full-stroke keyboard. For competitive reasons, the 800 was expanded from 16K to 48K without a change in price. Again we, the consumers, benefit from the fierce competition in the computer industry.

If your primary computer interest is gaming (other than adventure games), there's no reason to get an 800 if you have a 400 with 48K—unless for some reason you prefer typing in a "Y" in response to "Play another game?" on a keyboard rather than on a membrane pad. All games designed for the Atari computers can be played on the 400, 800, and 1200XL.

The 800 costs about $300 or so more than the 400. The price of an 800 has hovered around $700. Recently the price has dropped below $400, due in large measure to the introduction of the 64K Commodore 64®, which lists for $595 but can be purchased for as little as $250.

The 800 is suitable for word processing. An excellent program, in fact, is available from Atari. The display can be expanded to 80 columns with an optional attachment. The user has a choice of viewing the entire 80 columns or having a "window" on portions of the text and scrolling horizontally across the screen to read the text.

Dyed-in-the-wool James Micheners usually don't go for scrolling. But I've talked to professional writers who don't mind it at all. In fact, one noted computer magazine columnist swears by Atari word processing (but then he's also hooked on the games, so this may be a classic case of rationalizing).

The 800 can handle financial chores well. *VisiCalc®* is available for it, as are other spreadsheet programs. Without a numeric keypad, however, heavy number crunching can be onerous on the Atari computers.

Atari 1200XL ™

$460–900   64K standard

The 1200XL, announced in late 1982, is a fancy 800, with 64K. The 1200XL has a sleek, streamlined look and a side cartridge slot without the bothersome slot doors that are built into the 400 and 800. The 1200XL handles all 400/800 software. Many in the industry have expressed disappointment that Atari's new computer didn't incorporate more significant technological improvements over the 800.

It is probably not worth it for most people to spend the extra $100 or so for the 1200XL, since the 800 can be expanded to 64K for far less. Perhaps the 1200XL will appeal to a few millionaires who don't want their computer to clash with their Danish Modern furniture.

Chapter 15

Apple® IIe™

$1,300–1,400	64K standard; expandable to 128K

A fellow named Steven Jobs built the first Apple computer in his garage. He went on to form a multi-million-dollar company and to become a multimillionaire.

His computer was so popular that hundreds of companies started making products that could be used with it. These were not only programs (there are an estimated 20,000 Apple programs for sale), but also attachments that could be connected to offset deficiencies of the Apple or make it do things it couldn't otherwise do.

The more special products people developed, the more things the Apple could do. The more things the Apple could do, the more people bought them. Then more and more companies made products for the Apple. Eventually magazines published exclusively for Apple computer owners were formed and started competing with each other.

Even though the Apple has been surpassed by newer, sleeker, more powerful computers, it still enjoys a comfortable niche in the marketplace because its users can do so many things with it—thanks to all the support. The original model was called the Apple II™. This version was improved with a model called Apple II+™. Recently yet another version has been developed, called the Apple IIe™. (Perpetuating the use of computerese, the "e" stands for "enhanced." I guess "n" for "new" or "i" for "improved" would have been too comprehensible.)

You Should Buy One If:

A. You like some of the things the Apple can do because of its support—either software (such as *VisiCalc®* or one or more of the other 19,999 programs), or hardware, such as the music synthesizer board or the attachment that starts coffee brewing in the morning. You know the IBM Personal Computer™ is a better computer and will do all those things soon. But you want them *now*.

B. You want a computer that can help handle some of the tasks you do at work, but still want a system that can provide you with hundreds of exciting computer games.

C. All your friends have an Apple, and you want to be able to exchange or borrow software—or just be one of the crowd.

You Should Not Buy One If:

A. You don't know specifically what you want to do with a computer (better to start with a small inexpensive machine rather than invest from $1,300 to $3,000 in an Apple II system).

B. You would prefer to have a newer-model computer that can perform the functions you want done without plugging various types of boards into the Apple's slots to modify its capabilities.

C. Your primary interest is in game-playing or in word processing.

The basic Apple IIe (and its predecessors) leave a few things to be desired. It allows only 40 columns on the screen (although the computer can be inexpensively expanded to handle 80 columns), and there is no numerical keypad to facilitate the entering of large volumes of numbers.

The Apple II +, which, in its obsolescence, is getting cheaper by the day, has no lowercase letters, has only 48K RAM, and requires a more complex, expensive conversion to 80 columns.

Because of the enormous amount of support for the Apple, you can perform just about any function you choose on this computer. In some cases, the extra equipment you must purchase is far from inexpensive. Nearly all of the software and other equipment that works with the Apple II + can also be used with the Apple IIe.

The Apple was purposely designed to be versatile so that extras could be added. This in fact is a primary reason that the computer has become so popular in businesses and schools and at home. Unlike most computer consoles, the Apple console opens easily—the top just slips off. Inside are seven slots and several connectors into which can be fitted "boards" or "cards" to make the Apple do other things. These plug-ins allow such things as 80 columns, additional memory, the use of the CP/M™* operating system, playing music, and so on.

People react differently to this situation. Some say, "I don't want to add something here, add something there, and end up with a slipshod Rube Goldberg device."

Others say, "This system's great. It's flexible. I can

---

*CP/M is a computer operating system that allows software to run on numerous computers. About 5,000 companies are producing programs to run on the approximately 650 computers that can operate under the CP/M system.

add the features I want and personalize the Apple to my individual needs."

Software? Wow! Apple has printed an advertisement that makes this point dramatically. Across the top we see: "Will Someone Please Tell Me What an Apple Can Do?" Below, on two full pages, are printed in tiny letters a listing of over a thousand programs for the Apple, covering everything from agriculture to real estate.

There's an excellent book out called *The Book of Apple Software, 1983* (it's annual); I mentioned it in Chapter 9. It provides in-depth evaluations of hundreds of Apple programs. Take my word, if you own an Apple II, the best $20 you could spend would be for this guide.

The stripped-down Apple IIe sells for around $1,300. If you're looking for a bargain, you might be able to get an Apple II+ for around $800—they sold for $1,300 not too long ago.

Package deals are available if you buy an Apple IIe. Check out your local Apple dealer; you may be able to get a copy of *Apple Writer*™ or *Quick File*™ thrown in for a fraction of list price. *Apple Writer* is a word processing program made by Apple that allows 80-column writing. *Quick File*, also made by Apple, is a data filing and retrieval program of use primarily in businesses.

The dedicated game player will want attachments to allow color and the use of joysticks and paddle controllers. Game controllers are connected to the back of the computer (on the Apple II+, the top of the console has to be removed to connect and disconnect controllers).

With all the support, the Apple II computers are going to be around a long time. But keep your eye on IBM!

Chapter 16

IBM® Personal Computer™ (PC)

$1,300   16K standard; expandable to 512K

The IBM PC is the computer that out-Appled the Apple. It's powerful, sleek, and of excellent quality, and few doubt that it will become the most supported personal computer in history.

The IBM PC is not for game-playing or limited home use. But with the avalanche of software coming out for it (the quantity is far below that for the Apple, but this will change rapidly), the IBM PC will be used for all sorts of things.

IBM, of course, has an impressive reputation, and the PC, as it's called (will IBM's future home computer be called the "HC"?), lives up to that reputation.

To give you an idea of the esteem in which the "*Itty Bitty Machine* Company" is held, an ad was placed— not by IBM—reminding us that "even the IBM Personal Computer™" needs software. That's like saying, "Even a Rolls-Royce needs gas."

You Should Buy One If:

A. You can invest $3,000 in a computer system, and you've found a word processing program (such as *EasyWriter II*™) or a calc that runs on the IBM and that fits your needs perfectly.

B. You're a phenomenal programmer, have some unique ideas for software packages that will benefit many potential users, and are looking for a way to earn some money.

You Should Not Buy One If:

A. Your primary interest is in games or small home uses.

B. You don't know what you want to do with a computer (either at home, in your business, or on your job). But you figure now that IBM has a personal computer, it's time to buy. Don't.

In a word, the IBM PC is superb. And it costs about the same as the Apple IIe™. Why would anyone buy an Apple? Because support for the Apple is far greater than for the IBM—now. But just wait.

The IBM PC is attractive and professional-looking; call it understated elegance.

The keyboard is generally acknowledged to be about the best personal computer keyboard there is. It has 83 keys, including a numeric keypad and ten programmable keys. It's detachable and light, so you can put it in your lap as you work. The keys click when you hit them, a feature deliberately put in by IBM to make the PC feel like a regular typewriter (some people don't like this).

The screen has 80 columns, and both uppercase and lowercase. And if you buy a one-color monitor (an extra $350) instead of using your TV, you'll enjoy the sharpest, clearest characters of any of the personal computers. The characters produced by most computers look like a series of dots (which is what they are). With the IBM PC, the characters look continuous, even though they're also little dots.

The screen characters are in decorator green, which makes it easier on the eyes.

With all these compliments, I've got to say something critical about IBM to show my objectivity. There *is* one thing—the keyboard has a peculiar feature:

If you type, you're probably used to having an oversized left shift key just to the left of the Z. On the IBM keyboard, that key is a slash (/); the shift key is one more key to the left, and it's the same size as the rest of the keys. No one can tell me why IBM did this. But it's not a serious problem; the average user gets used to it quickly.

You can buy a stripped-down IBM PC for about $1,300, hooking the computer up to your TV and using a cassette tape recorder. I doubt if many people do that, however. If you need the PC, chances are you need at least 48K and a disk drive and are willing to pop for a monitor as well. Now you're talking three grand.

In the infancy of the IBM PC (mid-1982—can you remember that far back?), users were crying for software. One fellow went so far as to write to a computer magazine, beseeching anyone who would listen to come out with entertainment programs for the PC.

A flood of software is now coming out. In fact, IBM is placing full-page ads encouraging others to write software for the PC; IBM will handle the marketing of it. This is a dramatic turn for IBM. The company used to be really high on what is called the "NIH Factor" (if it's *Not Invented Here*, it's no good). If you're interested, get a copy of *PC* magazine and look at one of IBM's ads; or write for information to IBM Personal Computer, External Submissions (their phrase, not mine), Dept. 765 PC, Armonk, NY 10504.

The PC has what is called a 16-bit microprocessor (all the other computers we're concerned with, except the TI-99/4A®, have 8-bit ones). A 16-bit computer operates on bigger chunks of data, which makes it faster.* The distinction between 8-bit and 16-bit machines is not important to most of us. (Yes, 32-bit machines are now being produced—mostly for expensive business computers.)

Many accessories are available for the PC, from IBM and the growing herd of companies that are jumping on the bandwagon. Expansion to 256K costs about $300. For $600, you can get the CP/M® operating system (described in the previous chapter) and expand to 64K; this opens up a huge library of programs for you to use.

The PC is an excellent machine for word processing and for using large *VisiCalc*®-type spreadsheet programs. The PC is also a good computer for game-playing, although color costs an extra $300 and there are not many games available. There will be, though.

Now you can even buy an IBM computer at Sears! The PC can be found at what Sears calls its "Business Systems Centers." It is also sold at Computerland stores in many cities around the country.

The PC is extremely versatile. As such, it is found in homes, in small businesses, and on the desks of executives who work for the country's largest companies.

The IBM PC is *the* personal computer today. As is always the case, it will someday be leapfrogged technologically. But that will be one huge jump!

---

*Strictly speaking, 8-bit computers can handle only up to 64K memory while 16-bit computers can have over 1,000K. You'll see advertisements for 8-bit computers claiming more than 64K capacity. This is made possible through a programming trick whereby only 64K memory is used at one time. Speed and efficiency are sacrificed doing it this way, but this is of no great concern to most home computerists.

Chapter 17

Commodore 64™

$250–595   64K standard

Many think that the Commodore 64, because it offers so much memory for so little money, was the reason that Atari® upgraded its 800 computer from 16K to 48K without an increase in price. All this competition makes me very happy. Keep it up, guys, we love it.

You Should Buy One If:

A. You want to compose music on a computer without spending thousand of dollars.

B. You're a programmer and
   —want to design computer games with sophisticated graphics, or
   —want about the cheapest 64K available.

You Should Not Buy One If:

A. You want a wide variety of games to play at home.

B. You want to do serious word processing.

C. You want a computer that is supported by large quantities of software in a variety of fields.

The Commodore 64 has an excellent keyboard, with a good, solid feel, an acceptable 66 keys, and both uppercase and lowercase. Game cartridges can be plugged into the console (but there currently are not many available).

The 64 has its weak points as well: only 40 columns across, and the characters, for some reason, appear fuzzy on the screen.

For a little extra, you can run CP/M™ programs on this computer (you must buy what's called a Z80 cartridge). There may be problems here, however, because many CP/M programs assume that 80 columns are available, and, as I mentioned, the 64 has only 40 columns.

The graphics (overall screen images, color and sound) of the 64 are superior. All this really means to most of us is that the games can be made to look and sound interesting. What it means to game designers and musicians is that they can do things on the 64 that can't be done on most other computers. For example, a music synthesizer is built-in. It has three voices, each of which covers nine octaves. The user can "shape" the sounds, by assigning values to four sound characteristics (musicians among you will know these are attack, decay, sustain, and release).

A feature called "3D Sprite Graphics" is also built-in. It allows the programmer to quickly design up to eight objects (aliens, cannons, etc.) by telling the computer what shape and color(s) he wants them to be. Commodore calls it 3D because each of the eight objects can be assigned a number to instruct it whether to pass in front of or behind the other seven (just like the monsters in the coin-operated *PAC-MAN*™ game do).

Commodore ads refer to the vast array of software that will be available. Note that I said "will be," not "is." Commodore has a tendency to use the future tense in product announcements. In anticipation of the 64's popularity, third-party companies are producing software for this computer. One outlet in New York offers 200 free cassette programs with the purchase of a 64.

As is the case with nearly all the computers discussed in this section, the 64 can be tied either to a television set or to a monitor. It operates with either a cassette tape recorder or disk drive (the latter costs about $400). Modems are available from Commodore for just over $100.

With some decent software support, the 64 might give both the Apple® and Atari computers a run for the money—our money.

Chapter 18

Two Portable Computers

Osborne I™

$1,295–1,795   64K standard

Ask the man on the street who the computer experts are today, and the chances are he'll say, "Why, Bill Cosby and Isaac Asimov. Who else?" (In case you don't watch TV or read magazines, Bill Cosby is an entertainer who does commercials for Texas Instruments. Isaac Asimov is a science fiction writer featured in TRS-80® Color Computer ads.)

There are two other men in the industry who know even more about computers and who have so much charisma that they're household words—in computer households, that is.

One is Clive Sinclair, the man who brought us the first computer we could all afford (the Timex Sinclair 1000™).

The other is Adam Osborne, writer, speaker, publisher, iconoclast, and creator of the Osborne I. The Osborne I was the first reasonably priced, reasonably powerful, and reasonably portable computer.

Osborne's is a great success story. In the first year of production, thousands of Osborne I's were sold. But nothing's certain in this life except death, taxes, and technological obsolescence. The Osborne I has been out-Osborned, as we shall see.

You Should Buy One If:

A. You travel a lot, need a computer when out of town, and must use the *WordStar*® word processing program, the *SuperCalc*™ spreadsheet program, or both.

B. You need a portable computer and can find an Osborne I on sale for much less than the cost of a KayPro II.

You Should Not Buy One If:

A. You have any interest at all in playing video games on your computer.

B. You're farsighted (referring to visual acuity, not ability to plan ahead).

C. You can find a KayPro II for the same price.

When it was first announced, the Osborne I was a dramatic technological breakthrough. For $1,800 you could own a 64K computer, with two disk drives, a built-in monitor, and software alone worth well over $1,000. And the whole thing folded up into a suitcase with a handle and fit under your airline seat. In putting this ingenious unit together, Mr. Osborne indeed was quite farsighted.

The Osborne I has a full-size keyboard with a separate numeric keypad. For some inexplicable reason, the keyboard has no "delete" key. This key is important when word processing with *WordStar*, the package included with the Osborne I. (When the delete key is struck, the character to the left of the cursor is automatically "erased"; I don't doubt that many users strike this key at least once for each line typed.)

It's very helpful that two disk drives are provided (two are needed to make duplication of diskettes practical). However, the capacity of the disks is limited (about 100K each), and many programs require more. Disk drives that hold twice as much (called "double-density") are available for another $200.

A battery pack is available (about $200), which allows you to operate the Osborne just about anywhere. There's also an attachment so the unit can be powered by an automobile cigarette lighter socket, for those who choose to do word processing on the road.

The Osborne I's Achilles' heel is that it has only a 5-inch screen. Although small, the characters are sharp and clear, and word processing on it is acceptable. You look through a 52-column "window" to see what's on the screen. The window scrolls back and forth across the 80 columns into which the text is formatted. When using *WordStar*, you may format the data so that complete lines are seen on the screen.

The software that is provided with the Osborne I is excellent:

1. *WordStar*, one of the best available word processing programs

2. *MailMerge*™, a program that allows you to address form letters

3. *SuperCalc*, an excellent financial spreadsheet program

4. CP/M™, the operating system that allows the use of the many CP/M programs on the market

5. MBASIC and CBASIC, two programming languages

Osborne took great pains to ensure that the user manuals were well written; they're even understandable, an unusual feature for computer manuals. This is probably because Osborne is a writer himself—a good one, in fact.

Does this computer sound good to you? Well...now read about the KayPro II.

KayPro II

$1,595–$1,795   64K standard

If you liked the Osborne I, you'll love the KayPro II.

You Should Buy One If:

A. You travel a lot and need a computer while on the road.

B. You want a low-cost computer with two disk drives for use at home.

You Should Not Buy One If:

A. You have any interest at all in playing video games on your computer.

B. Your primary interest is in child or adult education or in household programs.

The KayPro II corrects the basic shortcomings of the Osborne I and incorporates a number of other improvements as well. Below is a comparison of the two computers:

1. A 9-inch screen, which makes a *big* difference, since the total area of the screen is nearly four times that of the Osborne I's 5-inch screen

2. Disk drives with a capacity of almost 200K each (versus 100K each for Osborne disks)

3. 80 columns on the screen (versus the Osborne's 52)

4. Large, clear characters in eye-soothing green (versus the Osborne's small characters in black and white)

Most other important features of the two computers are about the same. KayPro II falls short in one category: Its manuals are incomplete and hard to understand.

Both the KayPro II and the Osborne I have 64K, fold up into an oversized attaché case, come with valuable complimentary software, and list for $1,795.

The free KayPro II software is impressive; it includes:

1. *Perfect Writer*™, a fine word processor
2. *Perfect Speller*™, an adequate spelling checker
3. *Perfect Calc*™, an adequate spreadsheet program
4. CP/M, a valuable operating system

I doubt if there are many in the industry who thought a few years back that it would be possible to buy a perfectly acceptable word processing package—hardware, software, and printer—for less than $2,000, and be able to carry the computer around with you. But it is now.*

---

*The KayPro II, all associated software, and an Okidata 80 printer and cable were recently advertised for $1,999.

Chapter 19

Other Computers

There are a number of other computers that are worthy of mention, but do not currently deserve your serious consideration for one reason or another (e.g., inadequate software, more suitable to business than home use, not yet on the market). These computers are covered briefly in this chapter.

Radio Shack® TRS-80® Model III

This computer neatly combines a keyboard, monitor, and two disk drives into a single unit. It does not have color, and its games are bleak. There is little home software for this system, which is of interest primarily to businessmen. The cost is around $1,800 with two disk drives. An updated version, the TRS-80 Model 4, is also designed primarily for business use.

TI-99/2™ and Timex 2000™

TI and Timex entered each other's markets with two computers introduced at the January 1983 Consumer Electronics Show.

TI announced a computer that sells for below $100 and has better features than the Timex 1000™. Called the 99/2, the computer has a real keyboard (well, sort of; the keys are rubbery-feeling) and 4.2K, expandable to over 32K. The 99/2 will be of interest primarily to those who want to program.

Timex, in turn, has come out with the Timex 2000, which is about the least expensive 16K computer available ($149 list price). Timex also produces a 48K version for $199. The Timex 2000 has an actual keyboard, eight colors, and far better graphics than the Timex 1000. The company claims to have a wide range of programs for the 2000, but it will be a while before this computer has much software support.

Panasonic JR-200U

Well, it was just a matter of time. The Japanese have entered the home computer market with a fine machine called the JR-200U. It's got power and many nice features, but not much software.

The JR-200U has 32K, a keyboard with rubber keys, eight colors, and 32 columns on the screen, and it can play triad chords over five octaves. List price is now quoted at $350, but I'll make a bet that it comes out at a lower price. Compatible disk drives, modems, printers, and other accessories are promised for later in 1983.

Panasonic made a deal with a software producer, Datasoft®. We are told that thirty packages will be available, including a typing teacher, an "easy calc," a check writer, educational programs, and games, games, games.

Aquarius™

Mattel®, the maker of Intellivision™, has come out with a new computer system called Aquarius. It has 4K expandable to 52K, 16 colors, and a keyboard with rubberized keys. The theme underlying this product is simplicity. The sleek, attractive equipment resembles a toy more than a computer. Accessories include 4K and 16K memory expanders, a printer, cassette recorder, disk drives, and modem.

Mattel plans to produce a full line of Aquarius game cartridges, including some of Intellivision's most popular games. Also included are educational games, a Logo children's programming language cartridge, and calc, tax tips, menu planner, stock charting, and speed-reading cartridges. I tried the word processor. That one you can forget. The keyboard has only one shift key. Even worse, the spacing bar is on the side—and it's not a bar, it's a key!

Spectravideo SV-318

Spectravideo displayed a fine-looking system at the January 1983 Consumer Electronics Show. With a list price of $300, the computer, called the SV-318, has 32K expandable to 144K, a full keyboard with rubber keys, and a joystick built right into the keyboard (I had hoped someone would finally come out with this; it gives the player a game controller nearly as sturdy as those on the arcade cabinets). Spectravideo displayed an attachment that allows you to play all the Coleco games on the SV-318. A line of accessories is planned, including a printer, cassette recorder, disk drive, and monitor.

I was astonished at the Spectravideo graphics tablet. You may draw on it, and the screen automatically prints the images created. You may select from one of 26 colors and change colors at any time. This is true electronic doodling. (I wish I'd had this product during all those boring Pacific Stock Exchange board meetings I used to sit through.)

Coming Soon?

Sony is planning a small 5K home computer to sell for $99, called the PHC 20, and a 16K unit to sell for $199. The salesman at the Consumer Electronics Show was vague and unfamiliar with the products, and the company didn't even prepare printed material describing the two computers. I'm not holding my breath until these come out.*

Ultravision tried something new. The company plans to sell, for $1,000, a 10-inch TV and 64K computer, with keyboard, joysticks, and a set of earphones. Ultravision claims this unit will play Atari® VCS™ and ColecoVision™ games (you must purchase an attachment to do this).

Industry insiders say that IBM will introduce a home computer called "Peanut" to compete with Atari, Commodore, and Texas Instruments home computers. The computer will probably cost $600 to $750. You can rest assured that Peanut, if and when it reaches the market, will be an impressive home computer.

Lisa™ is Apple's new computer system, the result of three years of research costing $50 million. The system will sell for $7,000 to $10,000 and is designed for business use. Lisa deserves mention because it is a major breakthrough in computer technology. Instead of having to type in commands and responses on a keyboard, the user operates a "mouse," which is a small rectangular box not much bigger than a pack of cigarettes. The mouse is moved on any flat surface; its movement directs a cursor on the computer screen.

*You have to be careful at the CES. Many of the products somehow never get to market. Sometimes the manufacturers introduce products to test reactions. They quickly and silently withdraw their brainstorms when they see them eclipsed by someone else's.

Apple claims this system will be so easy to use (the computerist's term for this is "friendly") that the average clerk will be able to learn how to operate Lisa in less than a half hour.

Efforts are underway to adapt this type of technology to lower-cost computers. VisiCorp®, the makers of *VisiCalc*®, has announced a software "environment" called Vision™ that will permit the user to operate programs on the IBM PC using a "mouse." There's no doubt that dramatic developments will occur over the next several years to expand the use of this revolutionary concept.

Chapter 20

What Computer Should You Buy?

OK. We've been through all the candidates. Now it's time to summarize, so you can see at a glance what's likely to be the best computer for you.

The first table summarizes the prices of the computers. You'll note two capacity figures, measured in K. The first is the capacity of the stripped-down version; the second is the capacity to which the computer can be expanded—at extra cost, of course.

COMPUTER	PRICE		RAM	
	Seen as low as:	List	Standard	Expandable to:
Timex Sinclair 1000™	$ 40	$ 100	2K	16K
VIC 20™	80	300	5	70
Texas Instruments 99/4A™	100	200	16	72
Atari® 400™	80	300	16	48
TRS-80® Color Computer	200	300	16	32
Commodore 64™	250	595	64	–
Atari 800™	380	750	48	64
Atari 1200XL™	460	900	64	–
Apple IIe™	1,300	1,400	64	128
IBM Personal Computer™	1,300	1,300	16	512
Osborne I™	1,295	1,795	64	–
KayPro II	1,595	1,795	64	–

If you're just looking at power vs. price, the table shows that the Commodore 64 is a bargain. For under

$200, 16K is available on the Atari 400 and TI-99/4A. (The Timex 2000 [see page 161] has the cheapest 16K currently, but is not included on our charts because its limited software makes it of interest primarily to programmers.)

So much for cost and capacity. Now let's compare the color and sound of the computers, which are important in evaluating their game-playing ability. I'll also get into a more serious subject and compare the number of columns and state whether each has lowercase letters, two important factors in word processing. For the computers that have color, I rate them, just as on a report card: A (excellent), B (good), C (fair), D (poor), and F (flunking). The number of sounds is indicated.

COMPUTER	COLOR	SOUND	NO. OF COLUMNS	LOWER CASE
Timex Sinclair 1000	–	–	32	–
VIC 20	B	3+1	22	X
TI-99/4A	B	3+1	32	–
Atari 400	A	4	40	X
TRS-80 Color Computer	B	1	32	–
Commodore 64	B	3	40	–
Atari 800/1200XL	A	4	40	X
Apple IIe	B($)	1	40*	X
IBM PC	C($)	1	80	X
Osborne I	–	1	52	X
KayPro II	–	1	80	- X

Legend: – :   Does not have feature
          ($) :   Extra cost
         3+1 :   3 voices and 1 noise generator

*An 80-column "card" is usually provided with computer.

What does this table tell us? Atari takes top honors in color and sound, followed by 99/4A, VIC 20, and Commodore 64. IBM and KayPro II have the most columns for word processing, although the Apple IIe is easily converted to 80 columns.

Finally, I'm going to go out on a limb and attempt to rate the computers by how well they perform some of the more common functions. Remember, this is my opinion only. I've considered the capabilities of each of the computers and, in some cases, software that I know is available for various functions. New software (and hardware attachments) is coming out all the time, so don't take this table as gospel without looking into new products.

I've grouped the functions into games, word processing, home uses such as education and budgeting, and, finally, financial spreadsheets. The last category is primarily a business function, but it's such a prevalent computer use that I believe it should be included.

COMPUTER	GAMES	WORD PROCESSING	HOME USES	FINANCIAL SPREAD SHEETS
Timex Sinclair 1000	D	F	D	D
VIC 20	B+	D	C	C−
TI-99/4A	C+	D	C+	C−
Atari 400	A−	F	B	C
TRS-80 Color Computer	C−	D	C=	C−
Commodore 64	D	C	D	B
Atari 800/1200XL	A	C+	B+	B
Apple IIe	B+	B	A	B
IBM PC	C−	A	C−	A
Osborne I	F	B	F	B
KayPro II	F	A	F	B+

The above table shows why a computer that might be the best for one person may not be of interest to someone else. If you want games, Atari's the way to go. For word processing, it's IBM or KayPro II. Apple is great for home functions, and the IBM PC excels in financial uses.

Now the final step. I superimpose on this scenario price differences, resulting in this final table to help in your quest for your ideal computer.

If you want:	What Computer (or home video system) to Buy and You Can Spend:			
	Up to $50	Up to $200	Up to $1,000 *(disk)*	Over $1,300 *(disk)*
The best games and couldn't care less about anything else	Timex 1000 (only choice)	Atari 400	Atari 800	Atari 1200XL
Best games possible, but home uses are more important	Timex 1000 (only choice)	Atari 400	Atari 800	Apple IIe
Word processing, but want to play some games	No viable choice	VIC 20	Atari 800	IBM PC
Best home computing or small business use; forget the games	Timex 1000	Atari 400	Atari 800	IBM PC
Best word processing; forget the games	No viable choice	Coco*	Atari 800 or Commodore 64	IBM PC

*Coco's *Color Scripsit*™ is marginally acceptable for home writing. Quick Brown Fox's word processing for the VIC 20 is unacceptable with 22 columns. With the 40- or 80-column attachment, however, it's acceptable.

The choices are not as black and white as the table would lead you to believe. For example, for under $1,000, you have your choice of an Atari 800 with disk, or an Apple II+ (the older Apple model) without disk. The Apple II+ offers more software (now), but do you want to cope with cassette tapes? Or do you want to spend about $1,300 and get an Apple II+ with disk—or perhaps spend a little more and get an Apple IIe with disk?

If you want to word-process, you must have a printer. I have not included this cost in the above table. Happily, the price of printers, too, is dropping continually. A dot-matrix printer can be purchased for around $500. Letter-quality printers are showing up for around $1,000.

If you want to word-process at the $1,000 level (excluding printer) and games are of *no* interest, it's probably a toss-up between the Atari 800, using Atari's excellent *Word Processor*™, or the Commodore 64, using Commodore's *Easyscript 64*™. In both cases, the screen displays only 40 columns when you're writing, and the text scrolls across the screen horizontally. This is certainly a limiting feature, but many writers find they can live with it. Your best choice probably depends on which package you feel more comfortable working with; you'd be well advised to try them both. (The Atari is also supported by two other fine word processing programs: *Text Wizard*™ from Datasoft®, Chatsworth, CA; and *Letter-Perfect*™ from LJK Enterprises, St. Louis, MO.)

As you can see, you could use a computer to come up with all the options. (Perhaps someone will design a software package to tell us what computer to buy—but then what computer would we run the program on?)

You probably won't fit exactly in any of the categories in the above table. But at least you've got a lot of information to help you make an intelligent choice.

After you make your decision, don't pick up the phone and order the Lucky Selection. Be sure to try the computer out firsthand to make sure it "fits" you.

If you follow these steps, the chances are remote that you'll get an electronic white elephant. It's likely that you'll end up with a computer that you'll actually use, probably spend hours with, and, who knows, maybe even fall in love with.

Appendix:
Periodicals That Can Keep
You Up-to-Date

Without doubt, the best way to stay current on what's happening in the field of home computers is to read magazines on the subject. Many have articles on software evaluations and new products. Some of the most informative material is in the ads for hardware, software, and new services.

Computer magazines are proliferating rapidly because of the exploding interest in (translation: sales of) computers. There are magazines for beginners (sort of), for well-versed computer hackers, for teachers, for writers, and for owners of specific computers. Here's a rundown.

Easy to Understand

It's difficult to find a home computer magazine for the rank beginner.* One publisher told me that such a periodical would be doomed to failure because readers would soon become knowledgeable and progress to more advanced magazines.

While this may be true, it is also true that most of us—especially adults—are intimidated by computers,

---

*One attempt at this is called *Small Computers*, Hampton International Communications, Southampton, NY. The "premiere issue" is undated, and much of the information therein is outdated. It isn't clear if the publisher intends to continue to publish it.

and there is widespread misunderstanding about the subject.

There seems to be a crying need for simple, comprehensible information about home computers for the average person. I hope someone comes out with an up-to-date monthly magazine written solely for the computer neophyte.

The four most widely read magazines that are fairly easy to understand are:

Compute! The Journal for Progressive Computing
    P.O. Box 5406
    Greensboro, NC 27403
    Monthly; $20 per year

Articles of general interest; technical discussions; programming tips. Typical articles of general interest:

    Computers in the Home—1990
    How *Compute!* Readers Use Their Computers
    Is Your TV a Radiation Hazard?

Creative Computing
    39 E. Hanover Avenue
    Morris Plains, NJ 07950
    Monthly; $25 per year

Software reviews (emphasized); evaluations of new computers and accessories; book reviews; articles of general interest, such as:

    Game Software for the VIC 20™
    Art and the Computer
    How Will the New Tax Law Affect Computer
        Owners?
    The Personal Computer Industry—Potato Chips
        to Panty Hose

Personal Computing
    Hayden Publishing Company
    50 Essex Street
    Rochelle Park, NJ 07662
    Monthly; $18 per year

Uses of the computer at home; reports on new products; book reviews; answers to readers' questions; articles of general interest, such as:

SAT Tutoring Programs: Give Them an
   Incomplete

Hand-held Computers: More Than a Curiosity

Hardware (and Software) of the Month

Popular Computing

70 Main Street

Peterborough, NH 03458

Monthly; $18 per year

Review of new computers and other equipment; tips
on using and programming computers; interviews;
articles of general interest, such as:

Deducting Your Personal Computer from Your
   Taxes

Modems: Hooking Your Computer to the World

Advanced Word Processing for the Apple®

An Informative Weekly

InfoWorld

375 Cochituate Road

Box 837

Framingham, MA 01701

Weekly tabloid; $25 per year

Articles are often technical, but many are of general
interest; human-interest stories; developments in the
computer industry. Published primarily for people in
the computer industry, but of interest to computer
users as well. Typical articles of general interest:

13-year-olds Design Games for TI, Apple

New Software Announced for the Timex/Sinclair
   1000

Players Claim Games Release, Not Cause,
   Tension

IBM Drops Charges Against One of Its Former
Employees

Intermediate

Microcomputing
73 Magazine Street
Peterborough, NH 03458
Monthly; $25 per year
Technical articles; evaluation of new products; pro-
gram listings for games and other uses; computer-
game reviews. Some typical articles:
KayPro II—the Perfect Traveling Companion
Conquering the Cube (Program Listing to Solve
Rubik's Cube)
How to Keep Your Disk Drives Humming

Advanced and Technical

Byte
70 Main Street
Peterborough, NH 03450
Monthly; $19 per year
This magazine is huge—usually over 600 pages. Ar-
ticles are generally technical and of interest to those
with extensive computer experience. Typical articles:
Microshell and Unica: Unix-Style Enhancements
for CP/M
A Brief Introduction to Electronic Music
Synthesizers
Design Techniques and Ideals for Computer
Games
Dr. Dobb's Journal
1263 El Camino Real, Box E
Menlo Park, CA 94025
Monthly; $25 per year

For experienced computerphiles. Review of software and of personal and business hardware.

For Writers (Easy to Understand)

Word Processing News: A Writer's POV on Word Processing

1765 N. Highland Avenue #306-IW
Hollywood, CA 90028
Bimonthly newsletter

For writers who use word processors (POV is a movie screenwriter's term for "point-of-view").

For Teachers (Easy to Understand)

The Computing Teacher

Oregon Council for Computer Education
Eastern Oregon State College
La Grande, OR 97850

Articles on computers written for teachers at the elementary and secondary school levels.

For Businessmen

Interface Age

P.O. Box 1234
Cerritos, CA 90701
Monthly; $21 per year

The leading magazine covering small computers for business. Some articles are of interest to home users as well. Typical articles:

The Ten Most Talked-About Products of 1982
Finding the Right Word Processing Program
Who Says You Can't Take It With You? (A
  Roundup of Portable systems)

small Business Computers (sic)
  CN 1988
  Morristown, NJ 07960
  Monthly; $20 per year

For users of small computers in business. Covers accounting, word processing, financial modeling, and file and record handling.

For Users of Particular Computer Systems

Sync (Timex Sinclair 1000)
  39 E. Hanover Avenue
  Morris Plains, NJ 07950
  Bimonthly; $16 per year

For owners of the Timex, or its predecessors, Sinclair ZX80 and ZX81 (hence the title). Some articles are technical; some are not. Included are program listings that can be typed into the computer.

Commodore—The Microcomputer Magazine
  487 Devon Park Drive
  Wayne, PA 19087
  Bimonthly; $15 per year

For owners of VIC 20, PET™, 64™, and other Commodore products. Contains somewhat technical articles, program listings, advice on how to use Commodore computers, and new Commodore products. The magazine is published by Commodore and is thus less than totally objective. Its articles are of interest and useful, however.

Power Play Magazine (Commodore computers)
  487 Devon Park Drive
  Wayne, PA 19087

Published by Commodore for Commodore computer owners, this magazine is less technical than the one discussed previously and emphasizes game-playing.

Antic, The Atari Resource

297 Missouri Street
San Francisco, CA 94107
Bimonthly; $15 per year

Programming tips and listings; new products from Atari and third-party vendors.

99'er Magazine (TI-99/4A™)
Box 5537
Eugene, OR 97405

Published for owners of TI-99/4A computers.

Color Computer News (Coco)
REMarkable Software
P.O. Box 1192
Muskegon, MI 49443

Chromasette "Magazine" (Coco)
Box 1087
Santa Barbara, CA 93102
Monthly; $45 per year

This is a software-of-the-month-type service. Coco owners receive six to eight program listings on cassette tape each month.

80 Micro (TRS-80® computers)
80 Magazine Street
Peterborough, NH 03458

Published for users of Coco and other TRS-80 computers, this magazine contains program listings, software reviews, letters from readers, and stories on new products. About one-third of the magazine is for Coco owners (titles of Coco articles are helpfully printed in red in the table of contents).

Three Magazines for Owners of Apple Computers

Softalk
Box 60
North Hollywood, CA 91603

Monthly; $24 per year (one year complimentary to all Apple computer owners)

inCider (sic)
P.O. Box 911
Farmingdale, NY 11737
Monthly; $20 per year

Apple Orchard
910 George Street
Santa Clara, CA 95050
Monthly; $15 per year

Two Magazines for Owners of the IBM Personal Computer

PC: The Independent Guide to IBM Personal Computers
P.O. Box 598
Morris Plains, NJ 07950
Monthly; $27 per year
Focuses primarily on business uses of the IBM PC.

Softalk
Box 60
North Hollywood, CA 91603
Monthly; $24 per year (one year complimentary to owners of the IBM PC.)

Other Sources of Information

If you become interested enough in computers to start reading computer magazines, you'll automatically become aware of additional sources of computer information.

You'll read about computer clubs, user newsletters, and computer book clubs. There's even a weekly computer television show (*The Personal Computer Show*, 3740 Colony Drive, Suite 130, San Antonio, TX 78230).

My advice is to start by getting copies of one or more of the easy-to-understand magazines listed at the beginning of this chapter. In addition to learning a lot, you'll discover where to go for additional information.

Because of the phenomenal expansion of literature about computers, you'll find that you'll be able to carry your computer education as far as you want to.

What Does the Future Hold?

I usually don't make predictions. I'd rather "go with the flow" and adjust accordingly.

However, the home computer field is so uniquely dynamic that I'm willing to bet (and give steep odds) that three things will happen:

1. The hardware and software will get better—BE-YOND BELIEF.
2. The hardware and software will get cheaper—BEYOND BELIEF.
3. We'll be able to do things electronically that we primitive beings cannot even begin to fathom.

It's going to be exciting just to sit back and watch what happens!!

More Game Books from SIGNET